Marc Quinn

White Cube

Marc Quinn

Allanah, Buck, Catman, Chelsea, Michael, Pamela and Thomas

Allanah and Buck

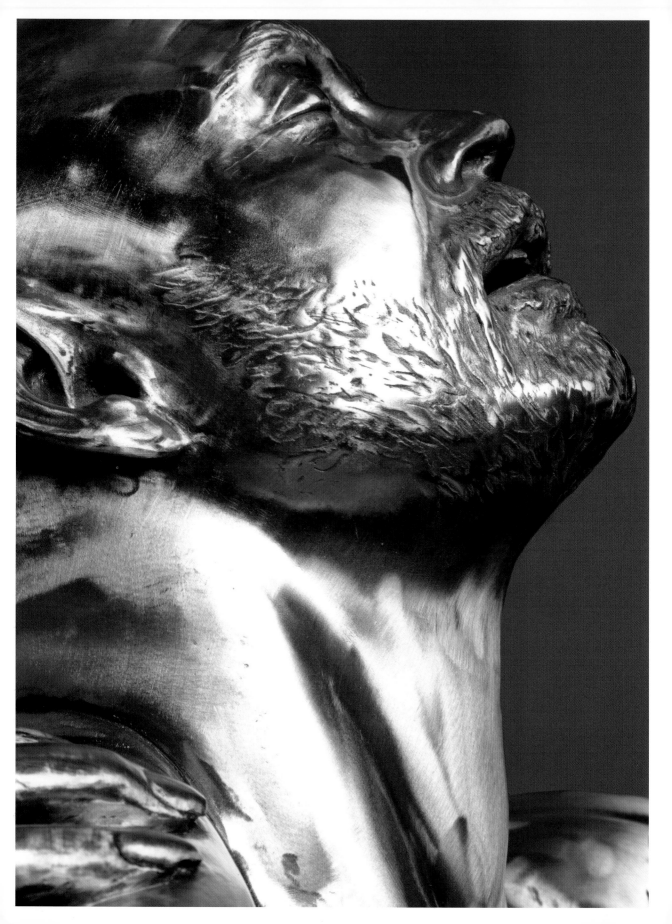

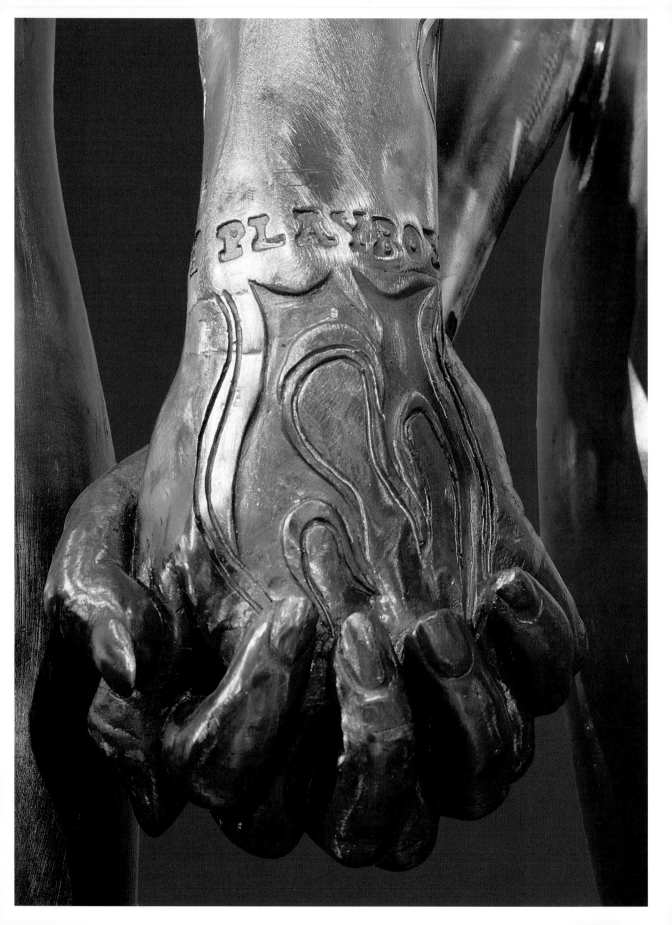

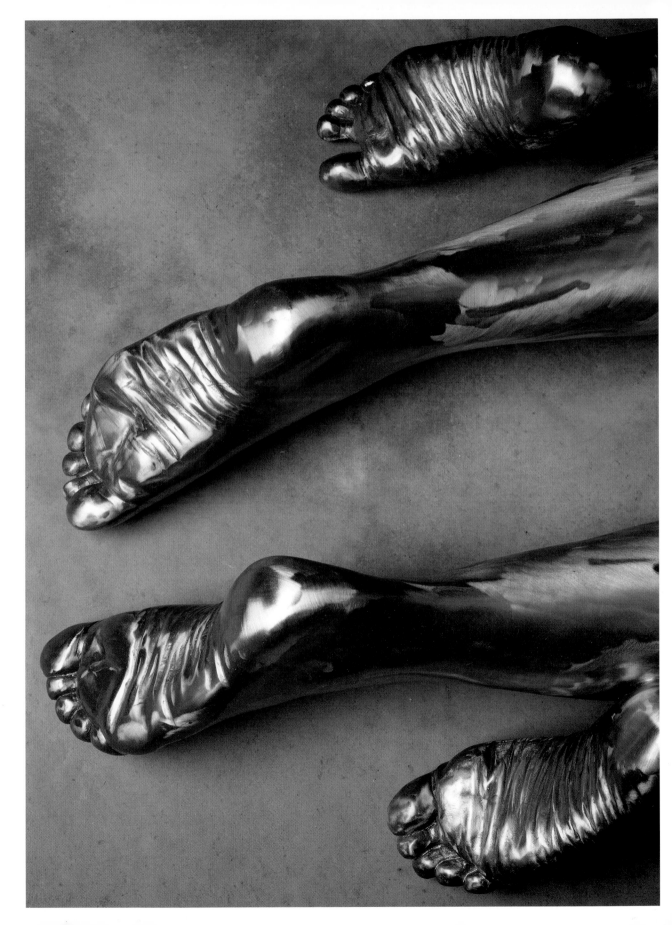

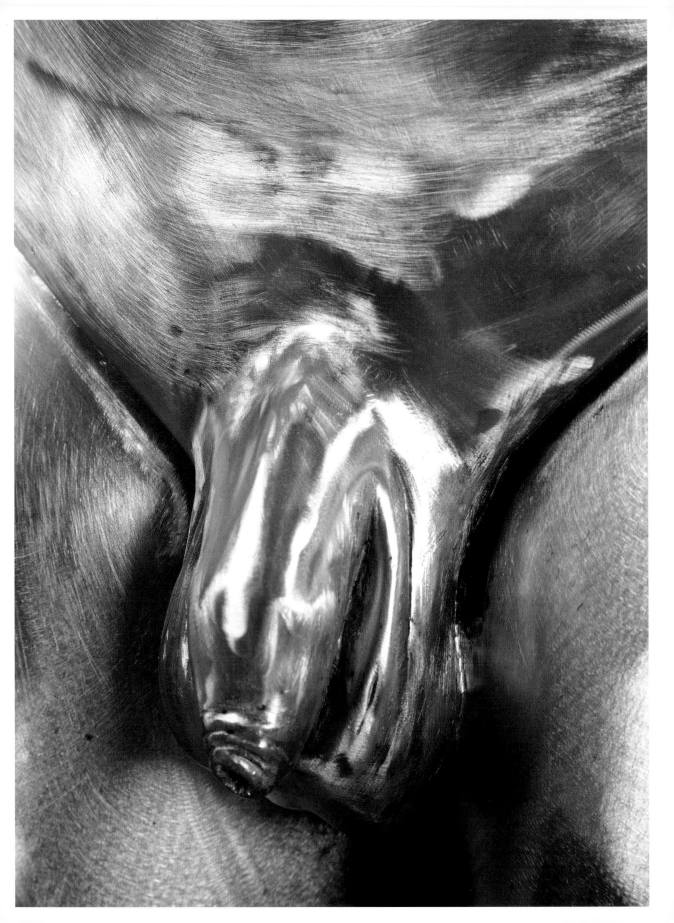

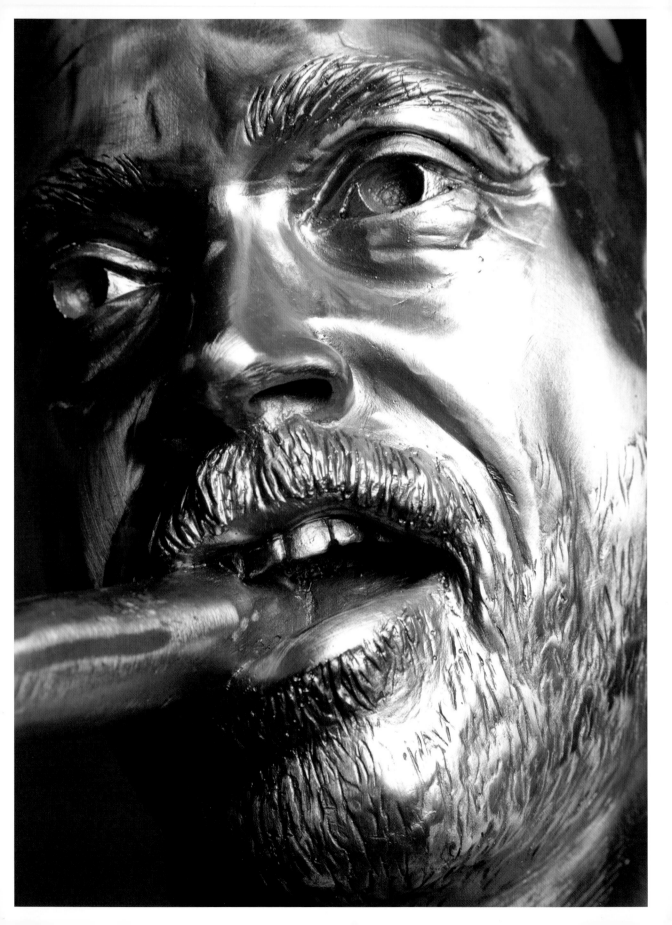

pages 10, 12–15, 19–21
Buck and Allanah
2009
Orbital-sanded and flap-
wheeled lacquered bronze
65 $^{3}/_{4}$ × 41 $^{5}/_{16}$ × 17 $^{11}/_{16}$ in.
(167 × 105 × 45 cm)

pages 7–9, 11
Allanah and Buck
2010
Orbital-sanded and flap-
wheeled lacquered bronze
48 $^{13}/_{16}$ × 59 $^{1}/_{16}$ × 24 $^{13}/_{16}$ in.
(124 × 150 × 63 cm)

pages 16–17
Buck with Cigar
2009
Orbital-sanded and flap-
wheeled lacquered bronze
65 $^{3}/_{8}$ × 27 $^{9}/_{16}$ × 16 $^{15}/_{16}$ in.
(166 × 70 × 43 cm)

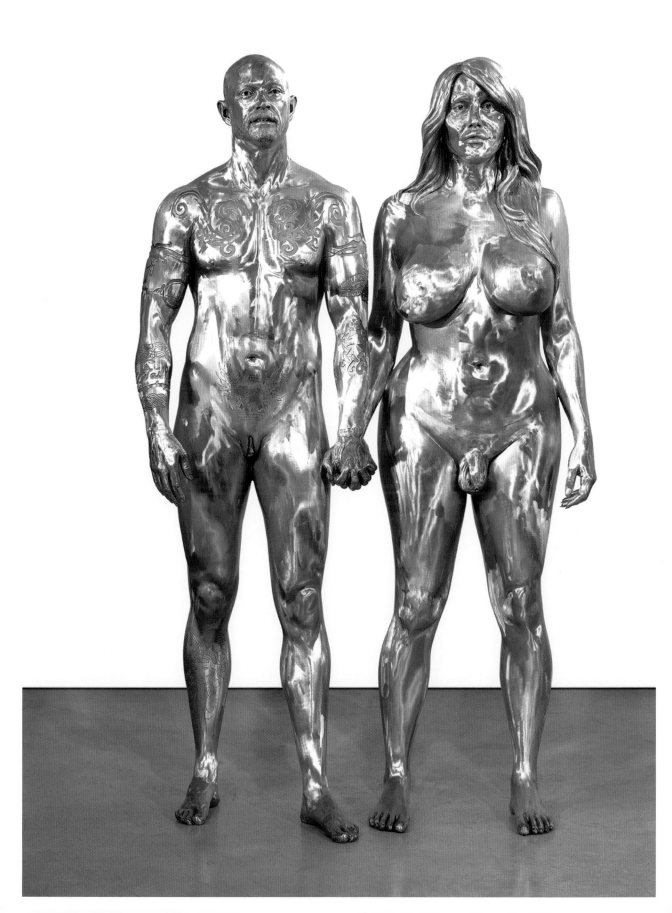

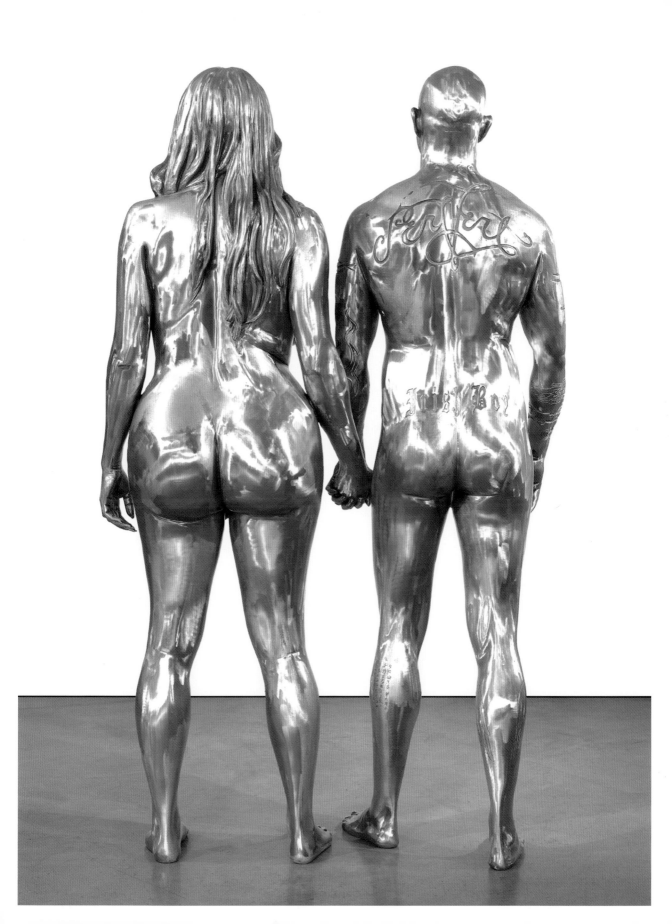

Allanah and Buck
2010
Orbital-sanded and flap-
wheeled lacquered bronze
48 $^{13}/_{16}$ × 59 $^{1}/_{16}$ × 24 $^{13}/_{16}$ in.
(124 × 150 × 63 cm)

Buck in Ecstasy
2010
Orbital-sanded and flap-
wheeled lacquered bronze
24 $^{7}/_{16}$ × 20 $^{1}/_{16}$ × 14 $^{3}/_{16}$ in.
(62 × 51 × 36 cm)

opposite
Buck with Cigar
2009
Orbital-sanded and flap-
wheeled lacquered bronze
65 $^{3}/_{8}$ × 27 $^{9}/_{16}$ × 16 $^{15}/_{16}$ in.
(166 × 70 × 43 cm)

opposite
Buck with Cigar
2009
Orbital-sanded and flap-
wheeled lacquered bronze
65 $^{3}/_{8}$ × 27 $^{9}/_{16}$ × 16 $^{15}/_{16}$ in.
(166 × 70 × 43 cm)

below
Buck as an Object of Virtue
2010
Sterling silver
24 $^{13}/_{16}$ × 11 × 7 $^{7}/_{8}$ in.
(63 × 28 × 20 cm)

Catman

pages 33–39
Catman
2010
White Bianco P marble
with Black Belgian marble
inlay, Carrara marble and
stainless steel
15 $^3/_4$ × 13 × 13 in.
(40 × 33 × 33 cm)
Plinth: 51 $^{15}/_{16}$ in. (132 cm)
Ø 9 $^{13}/_{16}$ in. (25 cm)

Chelsea

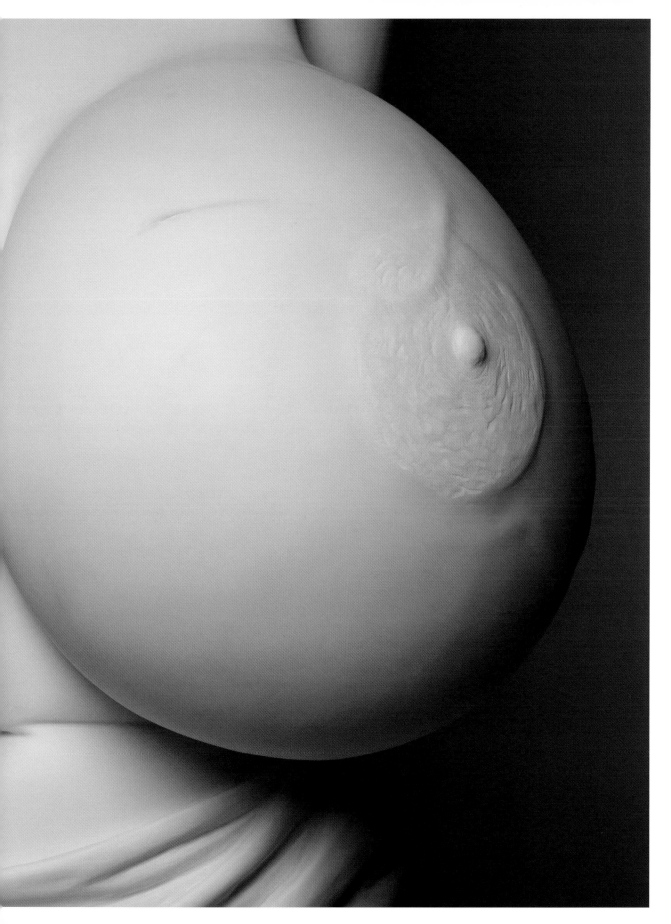

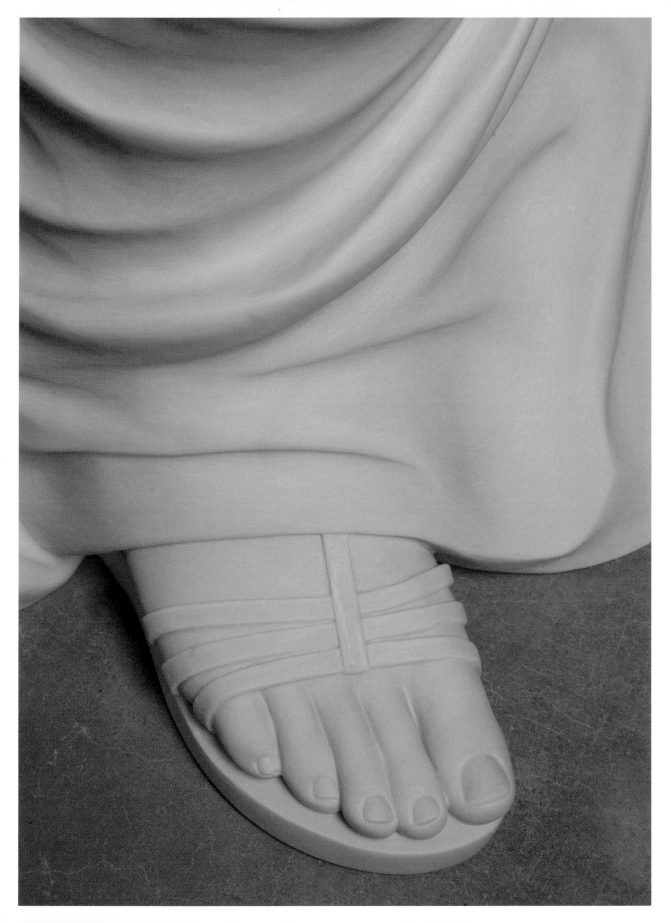

pages 41–52
Chelsea Charms
2010
Bianco P marble
66 3/4 × 23 1/4 × 20 1/2 in.
(169.5 × 59 × 52 cm)

below
Chelsea Charms
2010
Glass-beaded bronze
24 5/8 × 10 13/16 × 7 7/8 in.
(62.5 × 27.5 × 20 cm)

Michael

Man in the Mirror
(Monochrome Reversal)
2010
White Bianco P marble
and Black Belgian marble
Head: 37 3/8 × 40 15/16 × 44 1/8 in.
(95 × 104 × 112 cm)
Hand: 27 9/16 × 16 9/16 × 11 7/16 in.
(70 × 42 × 29 cm)

page 64
**The Outer Reaches
of Inner Space
(Monochrome Reversal)**
2010
White Bianco P marble,
Black Belgian marble and
Carrara marble
11 $^{13}/_{16}$ × 12 $^{5}/_{8}$ × 11 $^{7}/_{16}$ in.
(30 × 32 × 29 cm)
Plinth: 51 $^{15}/_{16}$ × 11 $^{13}/_{16}$ × 11 $^{13}/_{16}$ in.
(132 × 30 × 30 cm)

page 65
**The Outer Reaches
of Inner Space**
2010
White Bianco P marble,
Black Belgian marble and
Carrara marble
11 $^{13}/_{16}$ × 12 $^{5}/_{8}$ × 11 $^{7}/_{16}$ in.
(30 × 32 × 29 cm)
Plinth: 51 $^{15}/_{16}$ × 11 $^{13}/_{16}$ × 11 $^{13}/_{16}$ in.
(132 × 30 × 30 cm)

opposite
Lunar Module
2010
Sterling silver
11 $^{13}/_{16}$ × 12 $^{3}/_{16}$ × 11 $^{13}/_{16}$ in.
(30 × 31 × 30 cm)
Base: 8 $^{1}/_{16}$ × 8 $^{1}/_{16}$ × 8 $^{1}/_{16}$ in.
(20.5 × 20.5 × 20.5 cm)

Pamela

pages 72, 73 and below
**The Ecstatic Autogenis
of Pamela**
2010
Orbital-sanded and flap-
wheeled lacquered bronze
64 $^3/_{16}$ × 40 $^9/_{16}$ × 30 $^{11}/_{16}$ in.
(163 × 103 × 78 cm)

Thomas

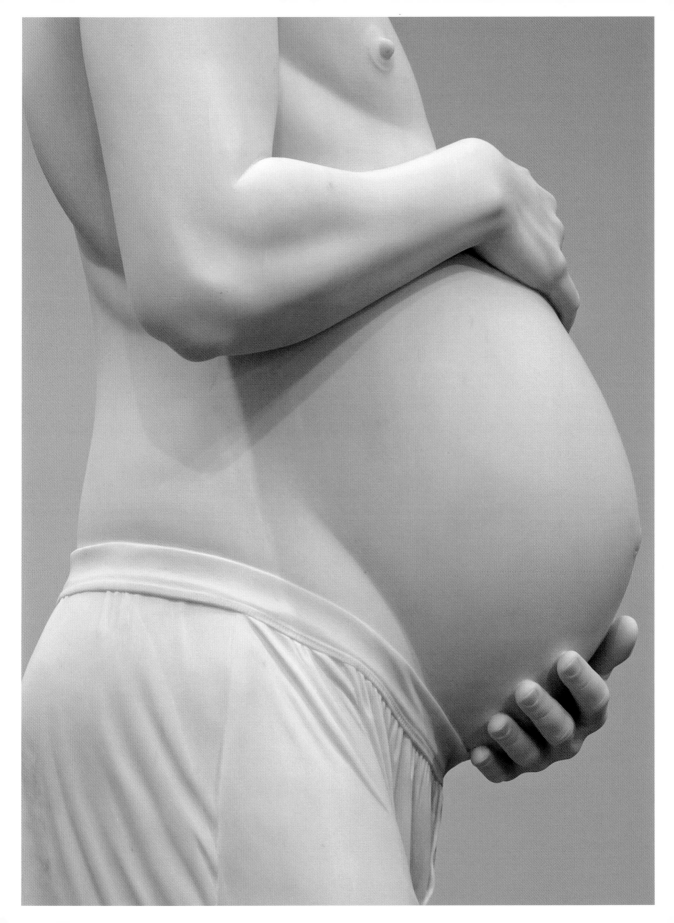

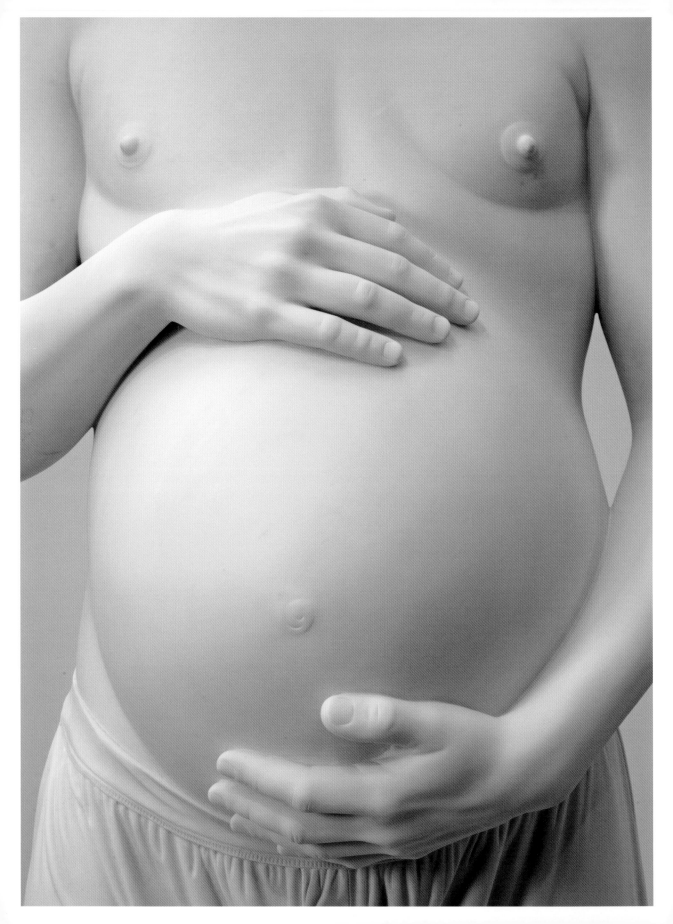

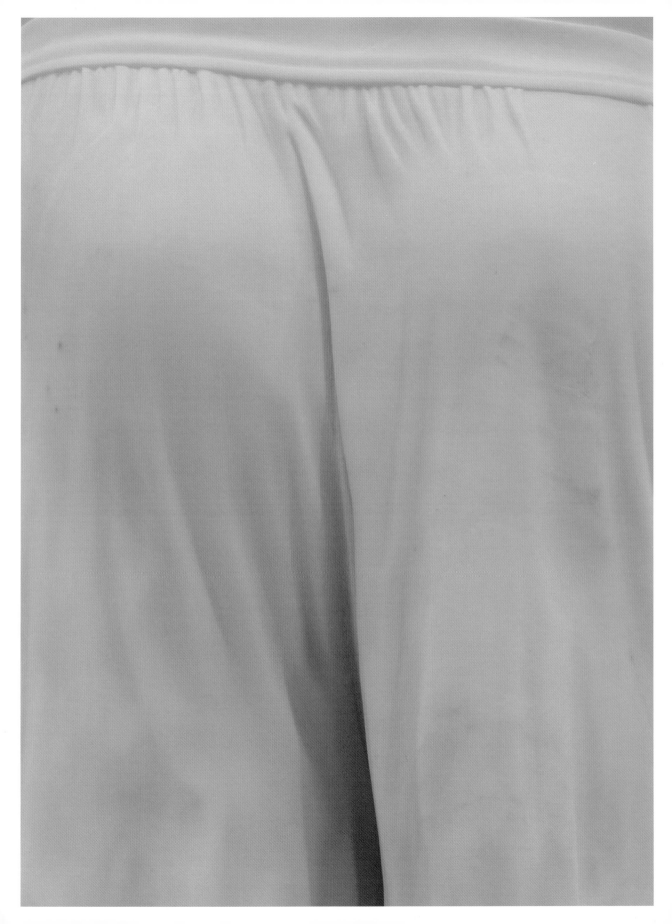

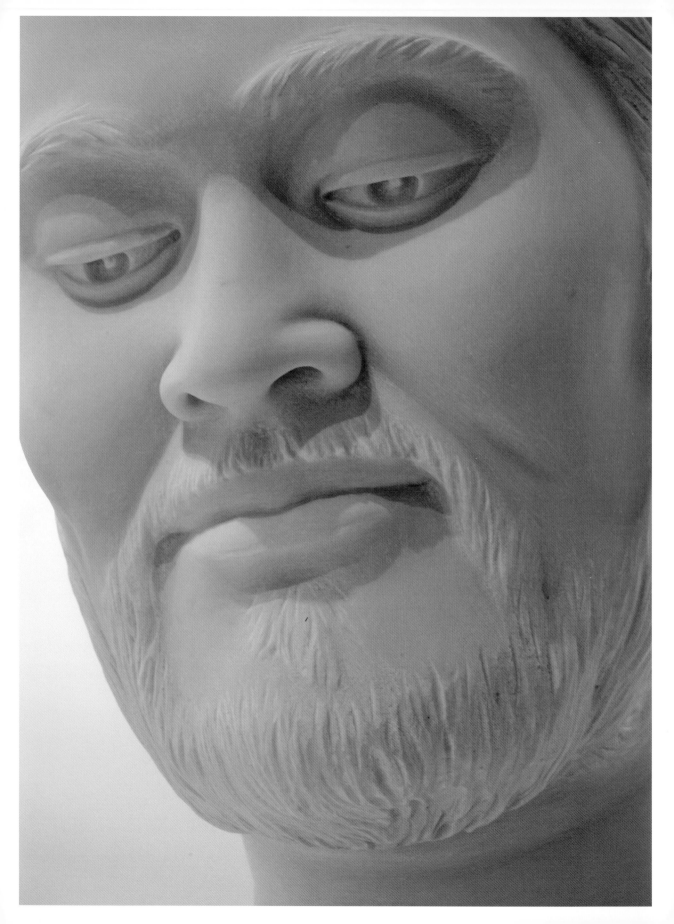

Thomas Beatie

2009

Bianco P marble

98 $^{13}/_{16}$ × 33 $^{1}/_{16}$ × 27 $^{9}/_{16}$ in.

(251 × 84 × 70 cm)

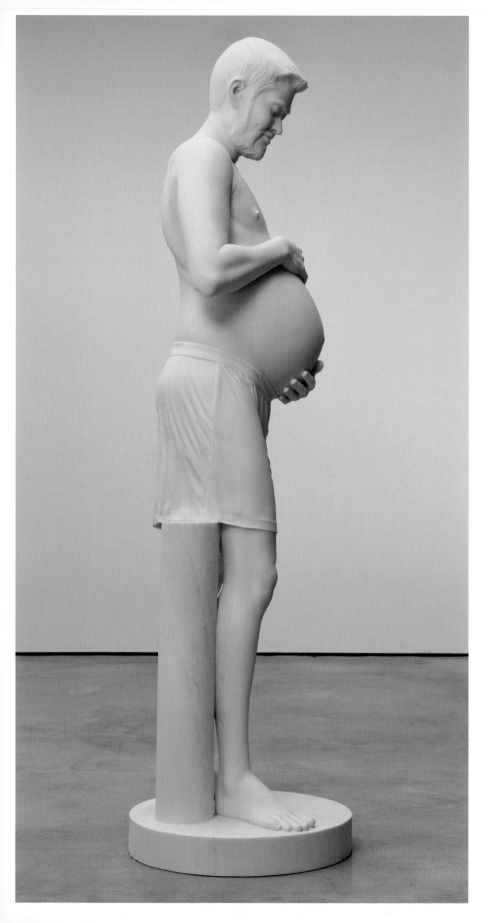

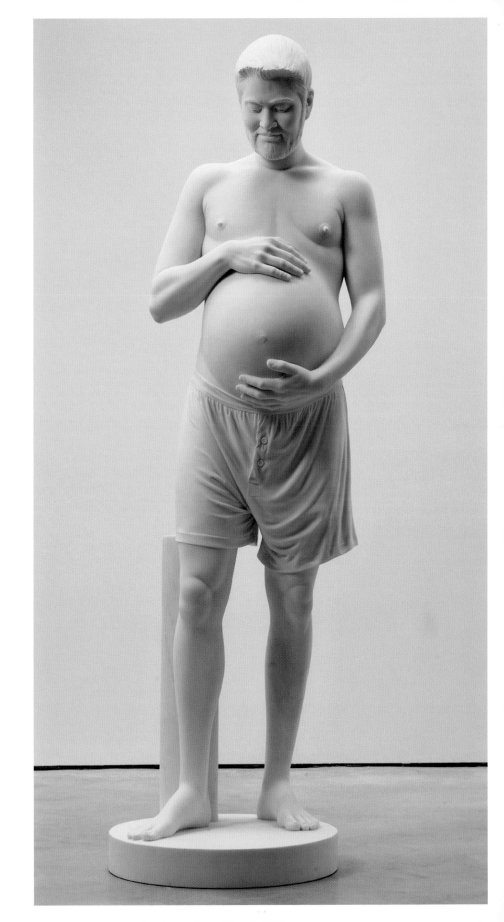

Reality Show

Joachim Pissarro and Mara Hoberman

Marc Quinn's latest series of sculpture-portraits, 'Allanah, Buck, Catman, Chelsea, Michael, Pamela and Thomas', opens a provocative new chapter in the artist's already extensive exploration of the relationship between corporeality and spirituality. Intent on debunking the conceit that one's physical appearance necessarily represents an accurate or even appropriate incarnation of one's psyche, Quinn has continually sought out subjects who exemplify an obvious disconnect between body and inner being. For example, 'The Complete Marbles' (1999–2001) comprises gorgeous, life-size sculptures depicting men and women with limbs that are missing or truncated due to birth defect, accident or necessary medical amputation. In this series, Quinn highlights the fact that, although physical deformities are not a symptom of intellectual weakness, we often view and treat the handicapped as if they are mentally challenged. Exploring the reverse scenario in 'Chemical Life Support' (2005), the artist presents men and women whose bodies appear perfectly healthy, but who are actually dependent on a variety of drugs to keep them alive. Through both of these series, Quinn illustrates that a superficial examination of a person's body often belies a genuine understanding of their true identity.

On a more personal level, Quinn's legendary autogenous self-portrait *Self* (1991) – a life-size cast of the artist's head made from five litres of his own blood – is further testament to the challenges (both physical and conceptual) involved in attempting to manifest one's inner spirit in absolute and tangible terms. *Self*, in its awe-inspiring presence, must be kept in a special refrigerated chamber. Its serene gravitas contradicts its inherently fragile and unstable materialisation as it highlights the numerous (and problematic) equations between blood (body), self and soul.

In his latest sculpture series, Quinn approaches the multidimensional construct of personal identity from yet another angle, asking whether people are more or less themselves after undergoing elective cosmetic surgery. His models are seven real people who have significantly modified their own bodies in an attempt to reconcile self-perceived inconsistencies between their inner beings and their natural external appearances. The unclassifiable, trans-corporeal experimentations of these seven subjects demonstrate an extreme experience of the body in constant flux. Quinn's subjects range from pop icons (Michael Jackson, Pamela Anderson), to tabloid favourites (Catman, Thomas Beatie a.k.a 'the pregnant man'), to niche-market porn stars (Buck Angel – a 'man with a pussy', as he is described on his official website; Allanah Starr, a self proclaimed 'she-male'; and Chelsea Charms, whose breasts are purportedly the largest in the world). Collectively, this group has undergone incredible physical transformations by a diversity of means including: plastic surgery, hormone therapy, tattooing, piercing, skin bleaching, hair-dying, all varieties of implants and transplants, not to mention intensive work-out programmes. While these 'surgery junkies' may initially appear freakish, they are quite literally, through the very flesh and skin of their own bodies, acute embodiments of the universal – and distinctly human – desire to control one's own physical appearance in order to accurately project one's true inner self to the world.

Heroically and sensitively depicted in white marble, gleaming polished bronze and cast silver, Quinn's bodies-in-metamorphosis illustrate calculated physical mutations that have been aided and abetted by modern medicine, pharmacology and extreme body conditioning. One of the most striking subjects is Dennis Avner – or 'Catman', as he prefers to be called. Catman has undergone numerous cosmetic procedures in a quest to externalise his feline spirit. His body is covered with thick black tattooed stripes; his teeth have been capped and filed into veritable fangs; his upper lip has been surgically bifurcated and reshaped; his ears have been pinned back; and he has fibreglass whiskers permanently implanted in his face. Catman's hybrid visage is certainly startling to behold – and it appears especially striking re-created in flawless white marble with black marble inlay – but it is clear that Quinn intends to engage the viewer beyond the initial shock and awe. Like all effective portraits, these works encourage us to look beyond

page 80
Catman Reversal (Purple)
2010
Oil on canvas
41 $^{7}/_{8}$ × 31 $^{1}/_{8}$ in.
(106.4 × 79.1 cm)

below
Buck Reversal (Blue)
2010
Oil on canvas
37 $^{3}/_{8}$ × 53 $^{1}/_{4}$ in.
(95 × 135.2 cm)

bottom
Buck as a Girl
2010
Oil on canvas
35 $^{13}/_{16}$ × 27 $^{3}/_{16}$ in.
(91 × 69 cm)

opposite
**Buck and Allanah
Reversal (Blue)**
2010
Oil on canvas
52 $^{3}/_{8}$ × 35 $^{13}/_{16}$ in.
(133 × 91 cm)

82

superficial characteristics and speculate about the persona within. What is peculiar and especially intriguing about Quinn's models is that their bodies and/or faces are to a large extent self-made. Quinn sees them as 'artists who use their own bodies as their media', and because their physical features are the results of psychological compulsions, the resulting portraits are disarmingly personal.

One of the most captivating aspects of this series is its illustration of the remarkable breadth of options by which it is possible to adorn or reform the body as a means of self-expression, exposing both the diversity of body-related fantasies and the wide array of procedures now available to successfully evolve these from fantasy to reality. Quinn, however, reminds us that while many of the physiques he has chosen to depict are taboo, there are certain types of makeovers that are already socially acceptable. A case in point is Quinn's full-length portrait of Anderson, an early endorser of plastic surgery, whose public persona is inextricably linked to her breast implants. Thanks in part to publicity from celebrities like Anderson, breast augmentation is now one of the staples of elective cosmetic surgery and represents a formidable source of revenue for cosmetic surgeons (who are statistically the highest paid of all medical practitioners). Anderson provides a good entry point into Quinn's portrait series for two reasons: first of all, the notion of a woman undergoing sugery to increase her bust size is more congruent with normative physical ideals than, say, the desire to make oneself look like a cat or to change one's gender; secondly, her implants are really not all that shocking by today's standards. Considering Anderson alongside Quinn's portrait of adult entertainer Chelsea Charms, whose breasts are impossibly enormous (according to Charms's own website, each of her breasts weighs approximately 26 pounds), it becomes clear how quickly society has acclimatised to the practice of sculpting, molding and recasting the human body. Given the relatively short trajectory during which breast augmentation has gone from being unthinkable to being a routine operation (the first silicone breast implantation was performed in

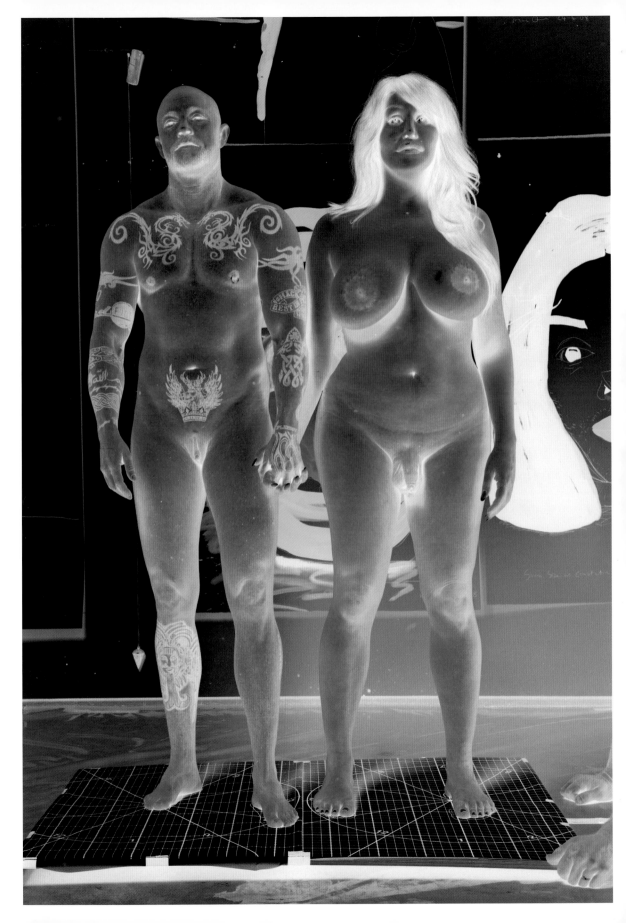

Chelsea Reversal (Pink)
2010
Oil on canvas
40 $^{11}/_{16}$ × 29 $^{13}/_{16}$ in.
(103.3 × 75.8 cm)

1962), it seems safe to assume that at some point in the not too distant future, Charms's body type – and by extension all of Quinn's models' physiques – will appear no more scandalous than Anderson's does today.

Quinn's masterful use of traditional materials such as marble and bronze offers affinities between his work and the finest examples of ancient Greek and Roman statuary. The Classical poses and life-size scale he favours, as well as the stylised anatomies of his models, are further indications of the artist's interest in comparing Classical notions of perfection with contemporary realities. While these art-historical references contextualise Quinn's sculptures, they also call attention to their powerful autonomy: whereas Classical representations of idealised physiques – enhanced musculature, exaggerated body parts, perfect symmetry – would have been unattainable by real men and women of that period, Quinn's anatomical depictions are based on actual superhuman forms. Quinn cannot be accused of exaggerating Charms's enormous breasts or Jackson's sculpted nose in order to promote a physical ideal. Quite the contrary, these extreme features lie at the crossroads between individual fantasy and the fully realised potential for transforming one's body.

The capacity to exert free will over one's natural physique to the extent that it becomes a viable medium for creative expression is epitomised by Quinn's colossal portrait head of Jackson (*Michael Jackson*, 2010). Perhaps the best-known celebrity 'surgery junkie', Jackson is depicted with one hand delicately brushing away hair from his iconic, mask-like visage. The gesture is familiar and quotidian, but it is also symbolic. Jackson's delicate fingers grazing his wholly 'unnatural' face highlights his self-transformation/mutilation and, seen in the context of Quinn's oeuvre, points to the autogenesis common to all of his models. In this respect, the portraits can be seen as referencing the work of 1960s and '70s avant-garde 'body artists' such as Michel Journiac and Gina Pane, whose art consisted of self-inflicted mutilations or of subjecting their bodies to extreme physical trauma. In the same way,

below
**The Ecstatic Autogenis
of Pamela**
2010
Plaster model

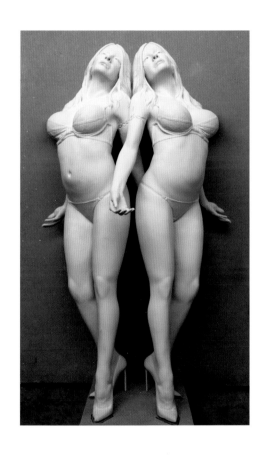

'Allanah, Buck, Catman, Chelsea, Michael, Pamela and Thomas' offers examples of contemporary 'body art' reframed within the context of Classical portrait sculpture. There is only one difference: Journiac and Pane were typically posing for groups of avant-garde aficionados – Quinn's models are re-posing as their newly transformed selves in front of the world.

Although Quinn's models are physically diverse – each one an emphatically unique self-creation – they are also all unambiguously human. Through gesture, posture and facial expression, the seven figures convey an empathetic combination of pride and self-consciousness. A good example is *Thomas Beatie* (2009), Quinn's larger-than-life sculpture in white marble of the tabloid sensation who first gained attention in 2007 for becoming pregnant while undergoing female-to-male gender reassignment (Beatie is now expecting his – or is it her? – third child). Wearing only boxer shorts and standing in an elegant contrapposto pose, Beatie embraces his/her substantially swollen stomach with both hands, signalling that – perhaps even more so than the millions who gawked at the photos in *People* magazine or watched his/her appearance on the television chat show *Oprah* – s/he is utterly in awe of his/her own quasi-miraculous condition. Beatie's cropped hair, prominent stubbly jaw line and manly chest stand in dramatically jarring contrast to his/her pregnant belly, and yet these ostensibly antithetical physical characteristics are integrated seamlessly by Quinn into a graceful form. Beatie's serene facial expression and tender posture are, above all, unmistakeably maternal, and in this way Quinn's portrait of Beatie manages to appear beautiful and regal, even while contradicting normative expectations.

The 'gender-bender' bodies observed and represented by Quinn (in addition to Beatie, there are the two transgender porn stars, Buck Angel and Allanah Starr) encourage a philosophical reassessment of how personal identity – our internal and external selves – can be honestly and adequately expressed. Given the numerous available means of transforming oneself, and given our capacity to defy traditional abstract notions of gender and sexuality,

below
Thomas Reversal (Buff)
2010
Oil on canvas
52 ³/₈ × 35 ¹³/₁₆ in.
(133 × 91 cm)

Quinn's presentation of atypical anatomies inevitably calls into question the validity of fixed, gender-based identification. Indeed the term 'gender' not only designates our sexual identity (ordinarily taken as immutable), but also refers to a fundamental grammatical rule by which we linguistically distinguish three genders: masculine, feminine and neutral. Several of Quinn's models challenge the inadequacies of such a rigid morphological system in relation to the ever-more complex and continuously fluid process of self-identification. How then can we best refer to Beatie, a perfectly convincing male – bearded and tall with chiselled pectoral muscles and beefy arms – who also happens to be pregnant? It is clearly not sufficient to use an epicene pronoun to refer to a human being: certainly Beatie, who is literally full of life and comfortable with his unique status, cannot be an 'it'. Therefore, what term can be used to designate Beatie, Angel and Starr? 'She-male', 'transsexual', 'transgender' – these words all have very specific connotations and describe particular anatomical combinations and psychological states that are not necessarily applicable to the unique situations of Angel, Beatie and Starr. In recent years, alternative pronouns such as 'ze' and 'zer'[1] have been proposed as replacements for the normative male/female linguistic construct, but these have not yet entered the mainstream. Regardless of how language develops in order to adequately characterise such a diversity of humanity, Quinn's work signals the urgent need to confront the current limitations of language with respect to the prescient political issues of human rights and self-expression.

Angel and Starr are both in transition – female-towards-male and male-towards-female respectively – and each possesses an odd combination of primary and secondary sex characteristics from both genders. Angel, who is bald-headed with a scruffy beard and moustache, has a brawny build, broad shoulders and a muscular chest; he/she also has a vagina. In one of Quinn's several portraits of Angel (*Buck with cigar*, 2010), his/her nude figure confronts the viewer unabashedly – hands on hips, one foot in front of the other, head cocked slightly, a fat cigar sticking out of the side of his/her mouth – inviting a prolonged and contemplative gaze. We do not need Freud to tell us that the cigar Angel holds provocatively in his/her teeth is a surrogate penis, and the prop serves to further emphasise the difficulty in parsing his/her identity based on traditional notions of gender and sexuality. Angel's confidence and machismo are palpable from his/her authoritative stance and dogged facial expression – even though his/her relatively short height evokes a slightly vulnerable presence. Starr, on the other hand, is a buxom, full-lipped, feather-haired bombshell with a penis. In one sculpture (*Buck and Allanah*, 2010), based on a still from a porn film starring Angel and Starr, the couple is shown having sex – Angel down on all fours and Starr penetrating him/her from behind. In another double portrait (*Buck and Allanah*, 2010), the striking pair stands nude, side-by-side, feet shoulder-width apart, hands clasped. Together, this heroic and empowered couple suggest a contemporised creation myth: a modern-day Adam and Eve story celebrating the loss of innocence as expressed through the radical options for self-expression in the 21st century.

To house his new Adam and Eve (and all of their kindred dysmorphic spirits) Quinn has created a contemporary Eden that is appropriately reliant on modern technology – an artificial environment that gives new meaning to the notion of 'the garden of earthly delights'. His new series of vibrant – almost hallucinogenic – paintings, 'In the Night Garden' (2010), depicts mixed arrangements of flowers that naturally would never be found in the same climate nor bloom during the same season. By placing tropical orchids next to country wildflowers, for example, Quinn emphasises how modern technology enables us to defy Mother Nature and create combinations according to our own aesthetic preferences. The highly mediated process by which Quinn makes his wholly synthetic works results in a wondrous supernatural setting wherein the sculpted marble and bronze figures appear very much at home. The juxtaposition of the floral paintings with the portrait–statues forces us to extend our appreciation of the contrived beauty of an

artificial floral combination to the 'bouquets' of atypical sex traits and other artificial physical characteristics embodied by the seven models. Quinn's utopian vision, in which flora and fauna are infinitely mutable and interchangeable, illustrates a thoroughly modern (or is it hyper-modern?) mythology wherein the human capacity to subvert nature is triumphant – a simultaneously empowering, beautiful and terrifying notion.

1. Creel, Richard, 'Ze, Zer, Mer', *American Philosophical Association Newsletters* (The American Philosophical Association 1997)

opposite
Buck and Allanah
2008
Ink, watercolour and
pencil on paper
60×40 in.
(152.4×101.6 cm)

page 90
Cat Hallucination
2010
Ink and pencil on paper
60×40 in.
(152.4×101.6 cm)

page 91
Michael as Constantine
2008
Ink, watercolour and
pencil on paper
60×40 in.
(152.4×101.6 cm)

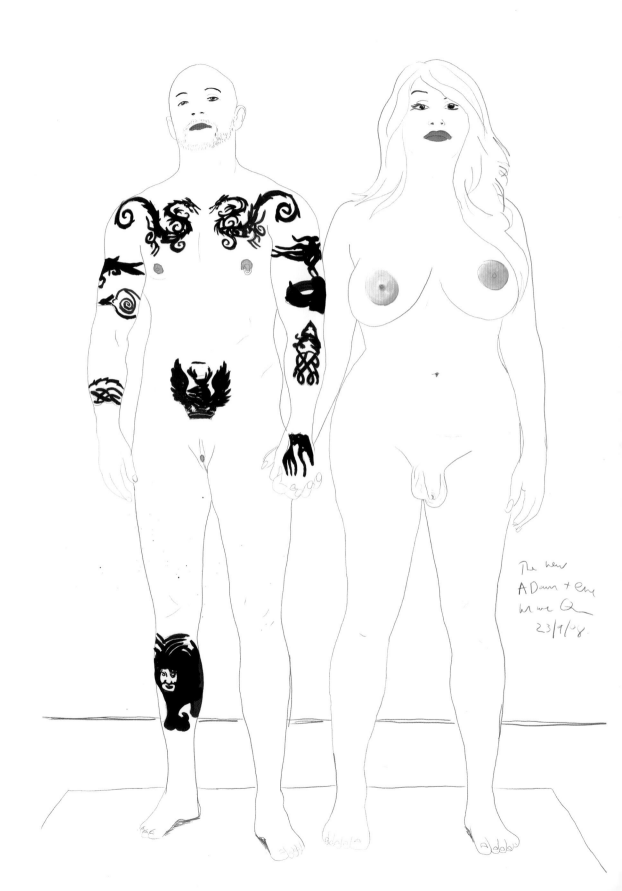

The New
Adam + Eve
We are One
23/9/08.

With Head?
muu Qui 26608.

left
Monochrome Reversal
(**White**)
2010
Ink and pencil on paper
40 11/16 × 29 13/16 in.
(76.4 × 56.7 cm)

right
Monochrome Inverse
Michael
2010
Ink and pencil on paper
60 × 40 in.
(152.4 × 101.6 cm)

left
Comedy and Tragedy
2010
Ink and pencil on paper
60 × 40 in.
(152.4 × 101.6 cm)

right
Smiley Ying Yang Mask
2010
Ink and pencil on paper
60 × 40 in.
(152.4 × 101.6 cm)

Seated with Fabric

MuQur 24'4 '08

14 in A
stue
+ Pinned?

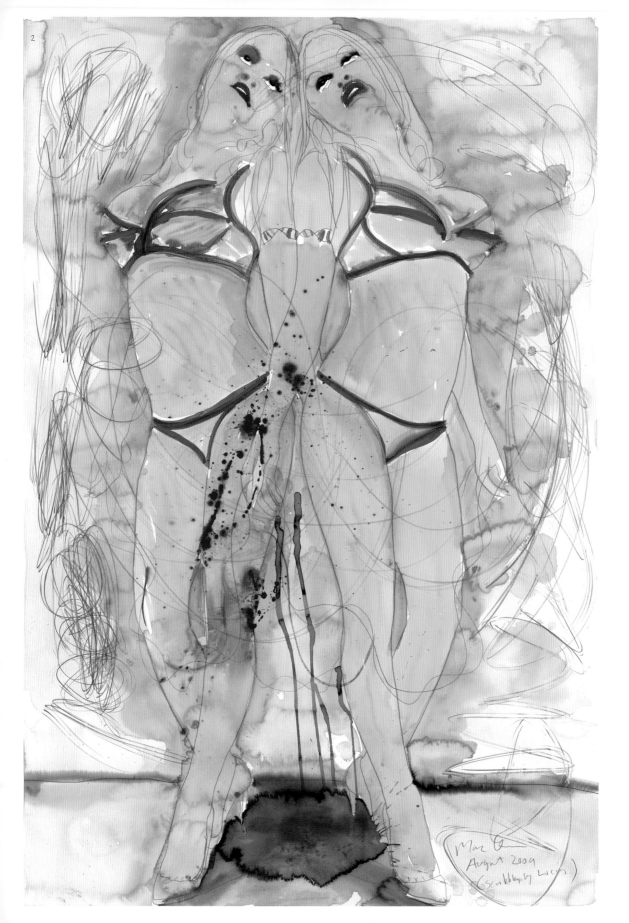

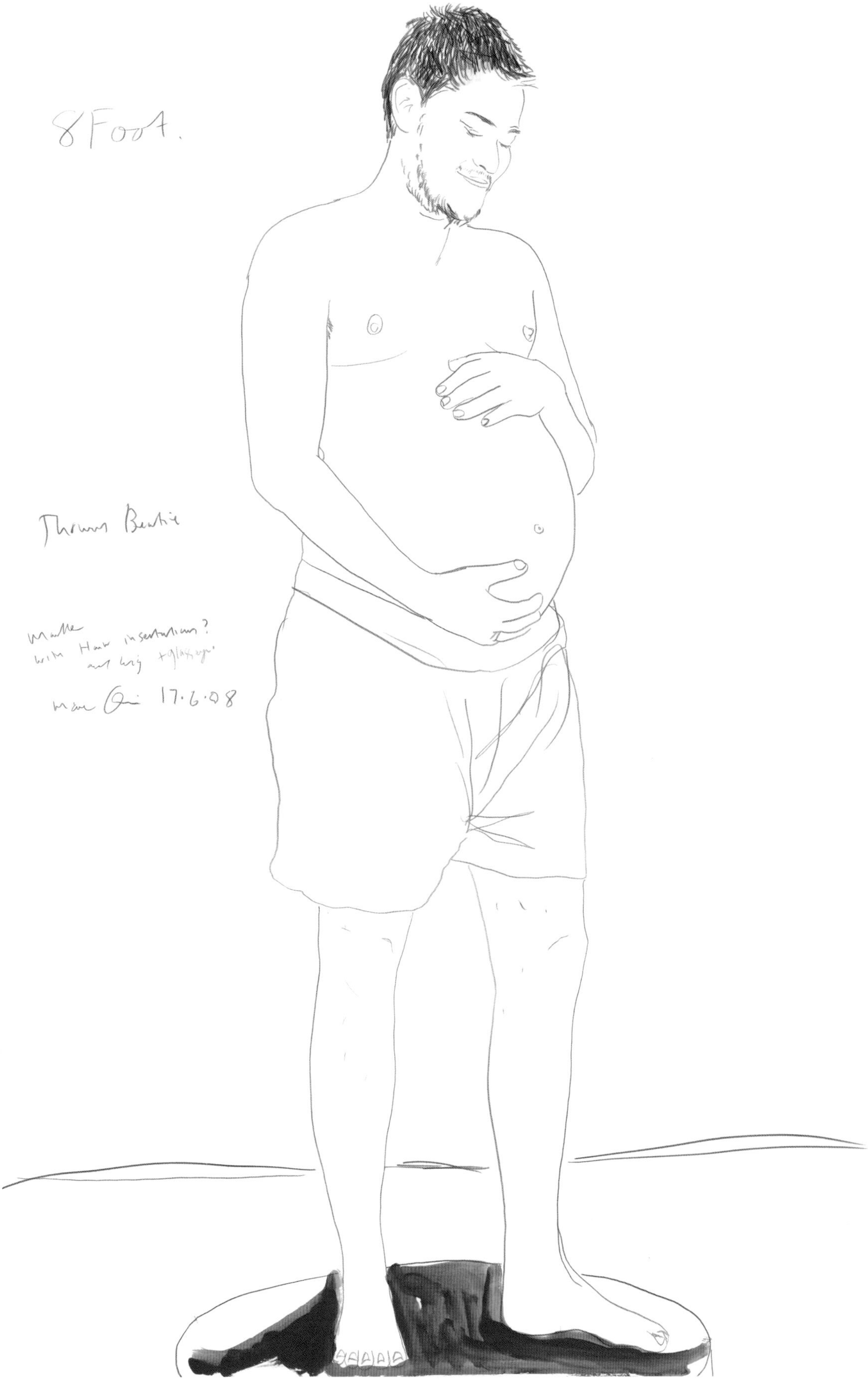

8 Foot.

Thomas Beatie

Maybe Hair insertions?
with Hair insertions
and long eyelashes

Marc Quinn 17.6.08

Fragmented Colossal
Statue of Constantine II
4th century
Palazzo dei Conservatori,
Rome

The Journey not the Destination

Marc Quinn and Joachim Pissarro in conversation

JP: **I wanted to ask you about this fascinating quote of yours regarding your latest series of portraits, 'Allanah, Buck, Catman, Chelsea, Michael, Pamela and Thomas': 'The new subjects are people who have decided in some way or another to take charge of their bodies and transform the outside to the will of the inside by surgery, and making their fantasy a reality. It is the first time in history that we have been able to transform ourselves to that extent.' I could not agree more.**

MQ: Because we're so used to plastic surgery being sensationalised, we forget the commitment people make to it. It's some kind of strange, warped, spiritual journey. Perhaps you can even argue that today, in Western society, it's the *only* spiritual journey one can undertake that lies outside of organised religion. It's a journey of transformation, one in which you take yourself out of the everyday into the realm of myth. These people make their dreams real; it's a reality show in the purest etymological sense.

JP: **And this fits your definition of the term 'artist'?**

MQ: They are artists in the sense that artists transform the outside world to reflect their own inner world. I would do this on a piece of marble or clay, on a canvas or using a computer, but these people apply it directly to themselves. *Self* (1991) was the closest I got to that, but I never wanted to permanently change my own body because, to me, being an artist is about changing all the time. These people are almost what you might call outsider artists except they use their bodies instead of traditional artists' materials.

JP: **You've also explored the work of tattoo artists, who likewise use the body as a medium.**

MQ: Yes, I think that tattoos are really interesting because they belong to the pre-surgery era. Tattooing is a way of marking nature with culture; it's a way of taking control of it, in the same way that ploughing a field or doing earthworks is taking control of nature. When tattoos were first applied they were informed by their cultural and religious context. Now, though, that context has been lost; now people invent their own contexts and things can go a bit crazy. It's like a thousand languages and a thousand religions all in the same place, with everyone starting from scratch instead of building on established traditions. Being tattooed is also about anchoring yourself in your body. When I think about the classic, non-tribal tattoo – the anchor on the sailor's arm – I think it's no accident that particular design rose to prominence. The sailor on his boat is trying to 'ground' himself using the tattoo, fixing himself within his body. Nowadays, people live such a virtual existence that it would almost be possible to live a life in which the body is hardly used. This makes our relationship to our bodies even more problematic – and more interesting. This is the area these latest portraits are exploring. The notable thing about Pamela Anderson – and what makes her unique in the context of this group – is that she is the only person using surgery within the parameters of cultural or tribal norms. Her transformation is well within the limits sanctioned by mainstream media culture. Anderson is like a tattooed Polynesian or a Makonde woman with a lip disc: completely acceptable. She shows us that equivalents to these rituals are still happening today within the context of our own 21st-century tribes.

JP: **You place significant emphasis on the spiritual journey, sometimes even the quasi-religious concerns, which animate your models – and presumably also animate you to a degree?**

MQ: Yes. I think that what I mean by being 'religious' is the attempt to make sense of life: the attempt to make sense of what it means to be a person in a body, to make sense of one's relationship to the world. I think that religion was invented to provide answers to these fundamental questions, so that people could get on with their lives and not have to think about them too much. If people are without a particular religion, then they start to invent their own answers.

JP: **So, are you suggesting that many of your subjects have taken it upon themselves to create a sort of toolkit of their own spiritual answers, which they have internalised.**

MQ: Well, in fact they've externalised them, because they've transformed their bodies. The journey might be to turn yourself from a man into a woman, or it might be to try to

The Expulsion from Paradise
Masaccio
c.1425
Brancacci Chapel, Church of Santa
Maria del Carmine, Florence

stop the visible effects of time. Obviously, there are lots of cultural pressures, and I'm not denying that many of those who have gone down this route may have done so as a result of psychological stress. These are stresses that everyone lives with, but the manifestations of how these people deal with them are far more extreme.

JP: I'm convinced by what you're saying, but to a more conservative audience what you are suggesting would probably at the very least seem paradoxical, if not downright shocking, because the people who traditionally look at and think about religious and spiritual values do not tend to associate this with transgender or transsexual practices.

MQ: Well, one has to remember that everything in human culture is a construct invented to satisfy the needs of a given moment in history and that just because it's been around for a long time doesn't make it any truer. At one point, Christian values were shocking to the pagans of Rome. I'm not saying that this approach to cosmetic surgery is a new religion, but I'm saying it's the same quest for the answers to the big questions addressed by great works of literature and art.

These people are working intuitively from within the cultural context they are part of, trying to deal with their physical transformation in much the same way as an adolescent might struggle with the transformation from child to adult. The other day, I was looking at the embryo sculptures that I made in 2008 and thinking, 'We all started off like that.' And the transformation from embryo to fully grown adult is much more extreme than anything that any of the models in this show have undergone. Throughout the course of our lives, humans transform to such an extraordinary degree that we almost pretend it doesn't happen, because if we actually stop and think about it, it's just too weird. So, having a breast implant operation is nothing compared to growing from an embryo into an adult. Every embryo starts off as female, but if it gets a massive hit of testosterone in the womb it becomes male. When we look at Buck Angel, we see that being played out in a small way on an adult body. But every man in the world has been on Buck's journey – in a much more extreme way.

JP: So, what you call 'the journey' is, in fact, a life journey.
MQ: It's the journey of the spirit in a body, I suppose, from birth to death; it also finds itself reflected in all the many little journeys in life.

JP: Staying with that great quote of yours, that these people are 'artists who use their own bodies as their mediums' – which we could almost use as an epigraph for this show – I'd like to bring up an example of a 19th-century artist who used bodies as his medium in absolutely every single work – all of his sculptures, drawings and paintings depicting dancers: Degas.
MQ: Yes, you're right.

JP: His model dancers were nobodies: they were the outcasts of society, considered the next best thing to whores. Well-to-do gentlemen would be waiting after the rehearsals to pick up young, new flesh – those are Degas' dancers. Socially speaking, we are talking about women that were truly 'low-life'. There is a certain element of that within your choice of subjects, as well, isn't there?
MQ: Well, obviously, some of the people I portray inhabit that world in order to make a living: Buck is a producer of pornographic films and, in fact, the sculpture of Buck and Allanah Starr having sex is a re-creation of a scene from one of their films. So you do have a sense of their outsider status. Yet, in the sculpture where they're standing holding hands, they're like a New Age Adam and Eve.

JP: So, between the porn stars and Adam and Eve is another subliminal journey.
MQ: It's the oldest journey in the world; it's the journey from the Garden of Eden to the incarnation. When desire enters the world, you are banished from the Garden: it's all about the 'before' and 'after'. These are classic themes that have been depicted many times over the centuries.

JP: Yes, such as in Masaccio's frescos of *The Expulsion from Paradise*, in which Adam and Eve are leaving the Garden of Eden. That's a wonderful example of before and after 'the fall'.
MQ: In a way, 'the fall' is a mythological invention to explain birth. The time before 'the fall' is the gestation in the womb, while being born is 'the fall' itself. What's interesting

with Buck and Allanah is that, because they also make pornographic films, you have this combination of the sacred and the profane, which has always been around: think of the temple prostitutes and the vestal virgins. Religion and sex are very much inter-related, even though we might not care to think so, and that's why I like the sculpture of Buck and Allanah fucking. To me it's like a Bernini: it has this sense that the moment of orgasm is the moment when you somehow free yourself from your bodily existence. That is what's so great about Bernini: he makes sculptures that are so ambiguous.

JP: You mean *Ecstasy of St Theresa*?

MQ: Yes, is she experiencing sexual ecstasy or religious ecstasy? Is there any difference between the two? It's all about transcendence – about momentarily leaving our bodies.

JP: Yes, exactly. Jacques Lacan, the French psychoanalyst, used the work as the cover image for one of his *Seminar* books.[1]

MQ: Well, I think psychoanalysis is another way of trying to deal with the same issues. For my subjects, you could say their transformation is a form of auto-analysis.

JP: I know you must be aware that your work is not exactly easy. Whether it's this present group of portraits, 'The Complete Marbles' series (1999–2001) or your self-portraits *Self* (1991–ongoing), your works are all pungent and loaded. The initial impression they give is very much one of being 'in-your-face'.

MQ: I'm always interested in challenging myself, and I'm not interested in things that don't make me think or feel. In creating the work, I go through the same journey that every viewer goes through, questioning what it's all about. I like to make art that makes you feel and makes you think. Obviously, I also like to make things that are beautiful. It's very interesting when you combine the two because beauty then becomes a sugared pill. Whether it's beauty of technique, execution or material, something a little more challenging slips in before you've realised it.

JP: I'm glad you brought up the notion of combining extreme, polarized emotions. I'm thinking now about

Rauschenberg, among other people, who created alluring and repelling works and displayed them simultaneously. For instance, when Rauschenberg was working on his gorgeous seductive gold-leaf collages, at the same time he was composing what he called 'Dirtscapes', literally a clump of mud, or dirt, laid out inside a frame. But you take this approach to another level – a human level – and that's even starker and tougher.

MQ: My feeling is that art should reflect the world we live in and the world isn't one thing: one minute it can be beautiful, one minute it can be terrible; one moment you can be happy and one moment you can be sad. I think that art is a mirror of life and so it should reflect all the nuances and facets, all the paradoxes.

JP: For those who are unfamiliar with your work, the question will be: 'What is this artist telling us; is he glorifying these people's transformations? What ethical stance is he taking?'

MQ: I'm just presenting reality – well, re-presenting reality. I'm not taking a moral view on it but on the other hand, of course, there's a celebration of humanity. I think what I'm looking for is humanity in areas in which people might immediately write off its presence; when, in fact, there is something there, a spiritual or a human interest.

JP: Your latest works strongly resonate, in my opinion, with the recent revival of Humanism in philosophy. The theorist Johann Gottlieb Fichte, probably one of Kant's best students, writes: 'The highest drive in human beings is […] the drive toward identity, toward complete oneness with one's Self, and, in order to be identical with one's Self, toward the unity of everything outside of the Self with one's own necessary concepts of it […] All concepts that lie in my Self should have an expression in the Not Self, a corresponding image. This is the nature of the human drive.'[2] Fichte defined mankind as 'nothing', by which he meant that mankind has the capacity to be nothing and to adopt all kinds of attributes to change himself in any number of ways. As he put it: 'Individuality is a reciprocal concept.' It's also about the notion

Ecstasy of St Theresa
Gian Lorenzo Bernini
c.17th century
Santa Maria della Vittoria,
Rome

The Venus of Willendorf
c.28,000–25,000 BC
Naturhistorisches
Museum, Vienna

centre
Princess X
Constantin Brancusi
1916
Philadelphia Museum of Art

right
Stoivadeion
c.300 BC
Temple of Dionysus,
Delos, Greece

that one receives one's own identity through another person's gaze.

MQ: Yes, exactly. These people are all about themselves, but they're also about communicating with the world, because their difference is only different in relation to other people's normality. So, they are very much operating within the social sphere, using the language of what is normal and abnormal in their work. After all, if they lived on their own on a desert island and had the ability to transform themselves in this way, would they make all these changes? I don't know, but I think they're reacting to the pressures of their social situation. What's also interesting is the way that they are re-making archetypes. If you go back to Ovid, to Greek mythology, you find this fascination with the transformation of one thing into another. Then you look at my sculpture of Chelsea Charms with her huge breast implants, and you could say she's like an extreme version of Aphrodite.

JP: Ovid's *Metamorphoses* does offer a marvellous example of what you are describing. Do you know *The Venus of Willendorf*?

MQ: It's a fantastic sculpture.

JP: Yes, this tiny piece of carved limestone with huge breasts. It reminds me of your sculpture of Chelsea Charms.

MQ: You also get that paradox where opposites meet, so you get the sense of her with her extreme femininity, her huge breasts, yet her profile could almost be that of male genitalia; the breasts are like two huge testicles. The same happens with Brancusi's sculpture *Princess X*: it becomes a phallic symbol, something that desires as well as being an object of desire. On the Greek island of Delos, I saw these sculptures of erect penises with testicles. The tops had broken off them, but they looked uncannily like the torso of Chelsea Charms.

JP: If one defines humanity as extreme elasticity or, to use a more art-related term, *plasticity*, then to be human is to be able to transform oneself. As you point out, one is transforming oneself anyway through the forces of life.

MQ: Well, in a way, all plastic surgery is a reaction to that. It's saying, 'I will *not* be transformed, I will be the transformer!' That's a very, very important motivation

and maybe that's what it's all about – making yourself the subject and not the object.

JP: I want to discuss further your definition of humanity with regard to your interest in Buddha, which is beautifully represented through your collection of Gandharan sculptures. In particular, I am thinking of that incredible example of the emaciated, starving vision of Buddha in your collection.

MQ: It's a paradoxical image. You have what appears to be someone on the verge of death, a cadaver even, when in fact it is the Buddha who has starved himself in an attempt, through austerity, to find enlightenment. It's a depiction of the moment he realises this is the wrong path and that he must now return to the middle ground. So, although it's an image that looks like death, it is in fact the image of the birth of the Buddhist religion.

JP: Buddha, who appears frequently in your work, incarnates extremes: he had been living a princely life, sheltered from the real world, and then he became aware of himself and reality. This awareness marks the beginning of every journey of self-transformation. That is why we see images of Buddha ranging from complete emaciation to the fat Buddha with a big belly.

MQ: What I like about Gandhara is that it's in-between; it's not Indian and it's not Greco-Roman, it's a hybrid of the first globalised world. And that's why, to me, it has resonance now, when we're living in this second globalised world in which everything is mixing up. It's also like the subjects of my latest portraits, who, apart from Jackson, are still in the process of transformation, as they will probably change their appearance again.

JP: Thomas Beatie is somebody who has undergone operations and is having hormone replacement therapy. When you made the portrait of him while pregnant, he was in the process of leaving one body, but stopped halfway through. He is almost like Buddha just before death. Thomas returns to his fertile female body shape, but in all appearances other than his belly he looks like a man. So he's neither identity, he's both.

MQ: Exactly. And yet Thomas would hate to think he looked

left
Bodhisatva
2nd century
Gandhara, Pakistan

below
Emaciated Buddha
c.2nd–3rd century
Lahore Museum, Pakistan

feminine, even though of course he is pregnant. When I originally showed him the sculpture I'd made, he was very careful to make sure that the breasts weren't too big and that it looked exactly like his body. He didn't want to be re-feminised in the sculpture.

JP: That is interesting, because I was actually going to ask you how someone like Beatie felt about this journey, which some transsexuals would consider a failure.

MQ: I believe it's about being something beyond categorisation. And I think that's what a lot of these people would say. Although it might seem like they're trying to be men or women, in fact they're not: they're just trying to be what they are, which is something in-between two worlds. What Gandharan art expresses culturally, they are experiencing in a personal way.

JP: Somebody had told me about your work, before you and I ever met, and they said: 'Marc Quinn is embarking on a series of sculptures of transsexuals.' It seems inevitable that this will end up being one of the labels given to the show but, in fact, nothing could be further from the truth.

MQ: I don't think labels matter. In a way, my whole point is that reality is beyond labels. Hopefully, it's more subtle, complex and varied than that.

JP: I notice that you use the terms 'he' and 'his' in relation to Beatie. I was talking with my colleague Mara [Hoberman] about the suitable vocabulary for someone like Beatie, so we started playing with language and genders and we came up with some hybrid forms: 'hir penis' or 'hes vagina', for example.

MQ: Well, in a way, language is a form of philosophy, isn't it? My subjects could be seen as concrete philosophers.

JP: Instead of just talking about theoretical language games, your models are living out these indefinable situations.

MQ: In a way, art is philosophy through the creation of objects, through reality.

JP: And objects that are actually living beings – human figures.

MQ: Be it abstract or figurative, to me all good art is

left
Ardhanarishvara
7th–8th century
Metropolitan Museum,
New York

below
**The Sleeping
Hermaphrodite**
Copy after a 2nd century
original
Louvre, Paris

essentially concrete philosophy. That's why the visual arts are so important right now: art compresses time and it talks about the world in a different way. It asks questions about where we are and who we are.

JP: Although you are using marble and bronze, there is nothing static in your work.

MQ: There's a tension created by using traditional materials to deal with things that are about flux and transformation.

JP: Exactly. It's the flux, the in-betweeness, which I find extremely interesting. In some of your portraits, you are representing situations that challenge the capacity of language to name the genders of the models who are inbetween masculine and feminine – and who, in fact, can be both.

MQ: I'm fascinated by the need we have to classify. Why do we care so much whether something fits into a system that we've invented in order to describe the world? When it doesn't, it causes a kind of short circuit, which makes you reconsider the whole notion of systems – which I think is a healthy thing.

JP: I'm trying to write about your work, but it is escaping and evading language by making categorisation virtually impossible.

MQ: That must mean it's working [laughter].

JP: Humour is a very important aspect when you're dealing with extremely complex issues.

MQ: I think there has to be a sense of beauty to art – and a sense of humour as well.

JP: Are you familiar with that incredible sculpture of the hermaphrodite at the Louvre.

MQ: Absolutely. There's also one in Rome, at the Musei Capitolini..

JP: With the sculpture in the Louvre, if you start to look at it from the rear, you see this very feminine, curvaceous back with a tapered waist. But then, as you move around to the front ...

MQ: You get a surprise.

JP: Yes, exactly. It's very dramatic and disorienting.

MQ: There's nothing new in the world about humanity, is there? [chuckles] We just re-make it.

JP: We find a new way of saying the same thing that fits within the context of today, the concerns of which are different from whatever was experienced before.

MQ: Well, every age is different and that's why we can re-make classic themes. My sculpture of Pamela Anderson is a kind of auto-birth. It's like the birth of Venus and the splitting of the atom; it's someone creating themselves. In the sculpture, only one of them has a belly-button.

JP: Let's move on to discuss your new series of paintings, 'In the Night Garden' (2010). I was rather surprised by the images of the works you sent me.

MQ: They are like pictures in reverse – more abstract, more dreamlike than regular compositions. These works form the landscape backdrop to the portrait sculptures. They are floral still lifes, composed in the usual way, which I then photograph and paint, after inverting the image's colours in Photoshop. The result is a sort of looking-glass world in which the focus of the flowers seems to fall apart and different images start to suggest themselves, as in a hallucination. They are like a daydream, an alternative reality, a strangely evolved nature; they are drugs for people who don't take drugs these days.

JP: How did this process of reversing the colour scheme come about?

MQ: It's a reaction to the transformation that's been taking place over the past year or two in the wake of the financial crisis, this sense of the world somehow going inside out or turning upside down.

JP: You explained to me that you completely make these up the arrangements of flowers yourself.

MQ: Yes. I go to the flower market in Covent Garden in London and buy flowers and put them together into a still life composition, take a photograph and then paint from the photograph. All the plants that you can buy in Covent Garden couldn't possibly be growing in the same place at the same time naturally: it's completely counter-seasonal. So, to me, the flower market is emblematic of the way that human desire has changed our relationship to nature. We have a much more fragmented sense of what is natural and what is unnatural. In 17th-century Dutch flower paintings, as each variety came into bloom, it would be added to the composition, so it would take the artist a whole season to paint a bouquet of flowers. In my paintings, you have the complete opposite: you have flowers that were immediately available and simultaneously in bloom in one place, in a cold, northern climate. In these reverse-colour images, everything that was black is white and everything that was white is black – although, of course, it's not an exact reversal; I always change the hues slightly while I'm making them. The effect is of a strange, futuristic dystopia. I went with my son to see the film *Avatar* the other day, and there is a night garden in the film that looks exactly like these paintings.

JP: In a way, your work for this show does bear a relationship to that film, doesn't it?

MQ: The film is about the humanity of the supposed outsider as opposed to that of the human. Like my sculptural works, it's about understanding the 'other'.

JP: How do you relate the paintings to the sculptures?

MQ: Well, they're also the product of a transformation, so they form an appropriate landscape for these figures to inhabit. The only difference is that this time I am the transformer.

1. Lacan, Jacques, *The Seminar, Book XX: On Feminine Sexuality, the Limits of Love and Knowledge* (Norton, New York 1998)
2. Fichte, Johann Gottlieb, *The Purpose of Higher Education*, (Nightsun Books, Mount Savage, Maryland 1988), p. 30 (translation modified)

below
Flowers in a Glass Vase
Ambrosius Bosschaert
the Elder
1614
National Gallery, London

In the Night Garden

**Hyper Nova
(In the Night Garden)**

2010
Oil on canvas
66 ⁵/₁₆ × 100 ³/₁₆ in.
(168.5 × 254.5 cm)

below
**Photoevaporation
(In the Night Garden)**
2010
Oil on canvas
66 ^{5}/$_{16}$ × 103 ^{3}/$_8$ in.
(168.5 × 262.5 cm)

pages 114–115
**Lavinia Plantia
(In the Night Garden)**
2010
Oil on canvas
66 ^{5}/$_{16}$ × 106 ^{1}/$_2$ in.
(168.5 × 270.5 cm)

The Kuiper Belt
(**In the Night Garden**)
2010
Oil on canvas
66 $^5/_{16}$ × 104 $^1/_2$ in.
(168.5 × 265.5 cm)

S Pectra I Line
[In the Night Garden]
2010
Hand-painted oil on canvas
66 ⁵/₁₆ × 100 in. (168.5 × 254 cm)

pages 118–119
Dickinson Crater
(In the Night Garden)
2010
Oil on canvas
66 $^5/_{16}$ × 101 $^{15}/_{16}$ in.
(168.5 × 259 cm)

below
Sepas Mous
(In the Night Garden)
2010
Oil on canvas
66 $^5/_{16}$ × 101 $^3/_{16}$ in.
(168.5 × 257 cm)

Glove and The Scream

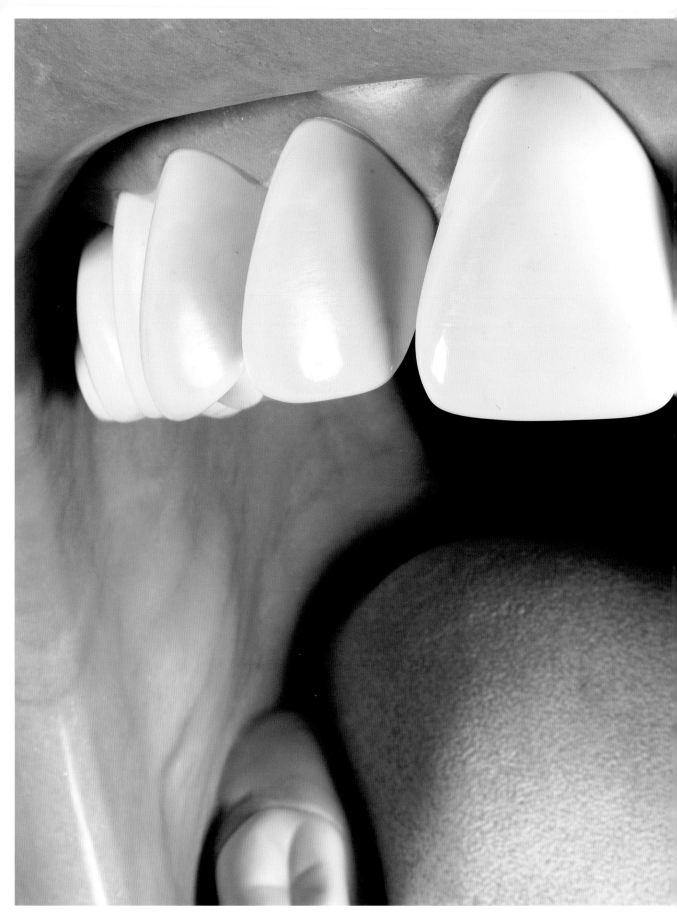

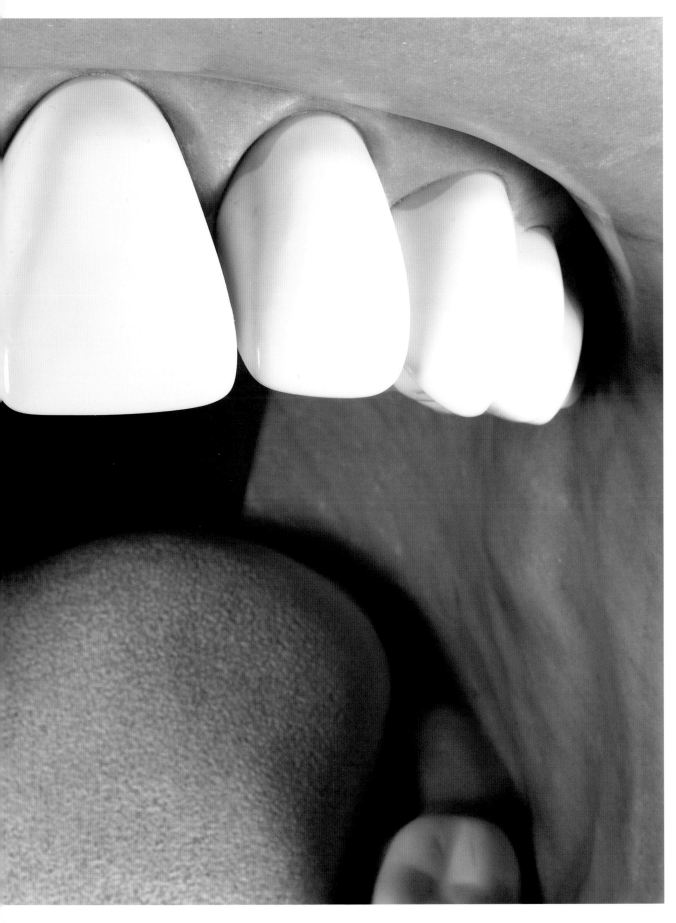

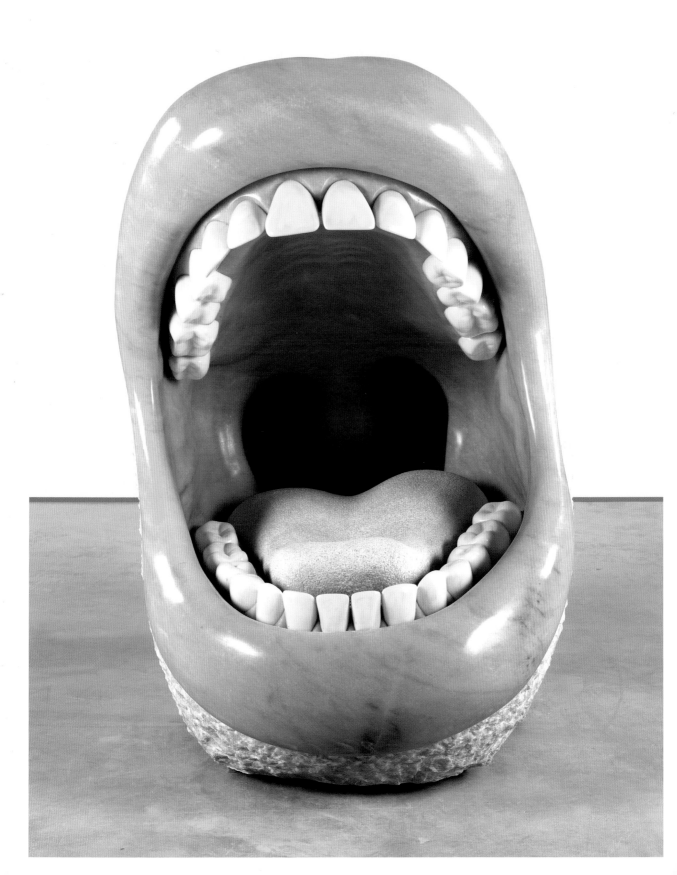

pages 127–129
Glove
2010
Bianco P marble
28 3/4 × 16 9/16 × 11 7/16 in.
(73 × 42 × 29 cm)

pages 130–133
The Scream
2010
Pink marble and Bianco
P marble
42 1/8 × 27 15/16 × 41 3/4 in.
(107 × 71 × 106 cm)

opposite
The Scream
2008
Watercolour, ink and pencil
on paper
60 × 40 in.
(152.4 × 101.6 cm)

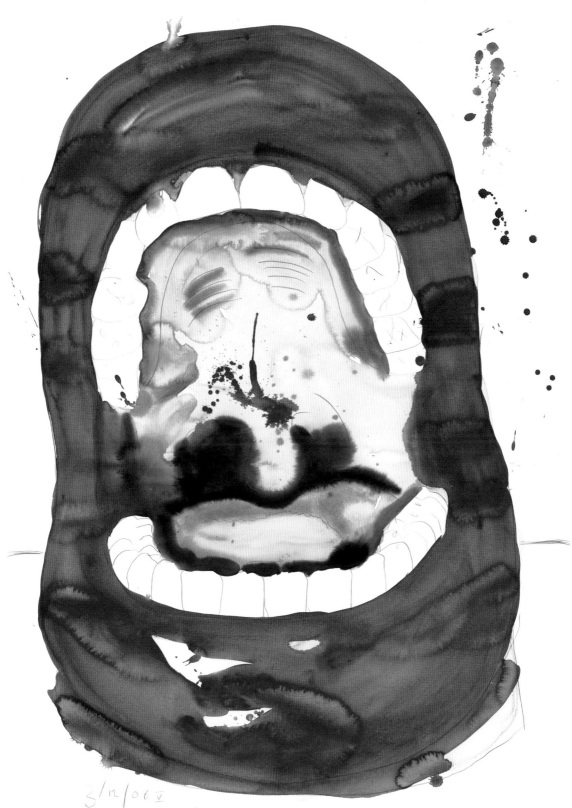

3/12/06 V
Big ref mouth (Scream)

Biography

– Lives and works in London
1985 – BA History of Art, Cambridge University
1964 – Born in London

Solo Exhibitions

2010 – 'Marc Quinn', Project B Milan at Patricia Low Gallery, Gstaad, Switzerland
2009 – 'Iris', Mary Boone Gallery, New York
– 'Marc Quinn', Goss-Michael Foundation, Dallas
– 'Marc Quinn: Selfs', Beyeler Foundation, Basel
– 'Materialise, Dematerialise', Galerie Thaddaeus Ropac, Salzburg
– 'Carbon Cycle', Galerie Daniel Blau, Munich
– 'Il Mito', Casa Giuleta, Verona
2008 – 'Evolution', White Cube, London
– 'Before, Now and After', Galerie Hopkins-Custot, Paris
– 'Marc Quinn', Gana Art Gallery, Seoul
– 'Alison Lapper Pregnant', The Forum, Rome
2007 – 'Marc Quinn', DHC/ART Foundation for Contemporary Art, Montreal
– 'Marc Quinn', Scolacium Archaeological Park, Catanzaro, Italy
– 'Sphinx', Mary Boone Gallery, New York
2006 – 'Paintings', Emanuele Bonomi, Milan
– 'Marc Quinn', MACRO Museo d'Arte Contemporanea, Rome
– 'Recent Sculpture', Groninger Museum, Groningen, The Netherlands

– 'Marc Quinn', Galerie Hopkins-Custot, Paris
– 'Chemical Life Support', Millesgarden, Stockholm
2005 – 'Marc Quinn', Galeria Guereta, Madrid
– 'Alison Lapper Pregnant', Fourth Plinth, Trafalgar Square, London
– 'Chemical Life Support', White Cube, London
– 'Flesh', Mary Boone Gallery, New York
2004 – 'The Incredible World of Desire', IBM Building, New York
– 'Marc Quinn', Atkinson Gallery, Millfield School, Somerset, United Kingdom
– 'Flesh', Irish Museum of Modern Art, Dublin
– 'The Complete Marbles', Mary Boone Gallery, New York
2003 – 'The Overwhelming World of Desire (Phragmipedium sedenii)', Peggy Guggenheim Collection, Venice
– 'Mirror', Power House, Memphis
– 'The Overwhelming World of Desire (Paphiopedilum Winston Churchill Hybrid)', Goodwood Sculpture Park, United Kingdom and Tate Britain, London
2002 – 'Behind the Mask – Portraits', Hatton Gallery, Newcastle
– '1+1=3 (Rainbow Sculpture)', Cammell Laird Shipyard, Liverpool
– 'Italian Landscapes from Garden 2000', Terrace Gallery Harewood, Leeds
– 'Marc Quinn', Tate Liverpool
2001 – 'A Genomic Portrait – Sir John Sulston by Marc Quinn', National Portrait Gallery, London
– 'Italian Landscape', Habitat, London
– 'Marc Quinn – Garden', Art of This Century, Paris

2000 – 'Still Life', White Cube, London
– 'Marc Quinn', Groninger Museum, Groningen, The Netherlands
– 'Marc Quinn', Fondazione Prada, Milan
1999 – 'Marc Quinn', Kunstverein Hannover, Germany
– 'Marc Quinn – Drawings', Sala América-Amarica Aretoa, Victoria, Spain
1998 – 'Incarnate', Gagosian Gallery, New York
– 'Marc Quinn', South London Gallery, London
1997 – 'Infra-Slim Spaces', Invisible Museum, SCCA, Kiev
1995 – 'The Blind Leading the Blind', White Cube, London
– 'Art Now – Emotional Detox – The Seven Deadly Sins', Tate Gallery, London
1994 – 'Marc Quinn', Art Hotel, Amsterdam
1993 – 'Marc Quinn', Galerie Jean Bernier, Athens
1991 – 'Out of Time', Grob Gallery, London
1990 – 'Bread Sculpture', Galerie Marquardt, Paris and Middendorf Gallery, Washington
1988 – 'Bronze Sculpture', Otis Gallery, London

Group Exhibitions

2010 – 'Realism', Kunsthalle Emden, Germany; Kunsthalle der Hypo-Kulturstiftung, Munich; Kunsthalle Rotterdam
– 'The Visceral Body', Vancouver Art Gallery, British Columbia
– 'Doppler Effect', Kunstahalle zu Kiel
2009 – 'Niet Normaal', Beurs van Berlage, Amsterdam
– 'Tears of Eros', Museo Thyssen-

Bornemisza and Fundación Caja Madrid
- 'Medicine and Art: Imagining a Future for Life and Love', Mori Art Museum, Tokyo
- 'A Tribute to Ron Warren', Mary Boone Gallery, New York
- 'Messiah', Modem Centre for Modern and Contemporary Arts, Debrecen, Hungary
- 'No Visible Means of Escape', Norwich Castle Museum, United Kingdom
- 'Assembling Bodies – Art, Science and Imagination', Museum of Archaeology and Anthropology, University of Cambridge
- 'Fuentes – Non-European Influences on Contemporary Artists', Galerie Thaddaeus Ropac, Paris
- 'Innovations in the Third Dimension
- Sculpture of Our Time', Bruce Museum, Greenwich, Connecticut

2008 – 'Love', National Gallery, London
- 'Out of Shape – Stylistic Distortions of the Human Form in Art', The Frances Lehman Loeb Art Center, Poughkeepsie, New York
- 'Genesis – Die Kunst der Schopfung', Zentrum Paul Klee, Bern, Switzerland
- 'Statuephilia – Contemporary Sculptors at the British Museum', British Museum, London
- 'Nothing But Sculpture – 8th International Sculpture Biennale', Carrara, Italy
- 'Open XI International Exhibition of Sculptures and Installations', Venice Lido and San Servolo, Italy
- 'Sphinxx', Stuart Shave/Modern Art, London
- 'Beyond Limits', Chatsworth House, Derbyshire, United Kingdom

2007 – 'Garden of Eden', Kunsthalle Emden, Germany
- 'Skin', The National Museum of Art, Osaka
- 'Six Feet Under', Deutsches Hygiene-Museum, Dresden
- 'The Naked Portrait', Scottish National Gallery, Edinburgh and Compton Verney, Warwickshire, United Kingdom
- 'Timer 01 – Intimità', Triennale Bovisa, Milan
- 'Genesis – Life at the End of the Information Age', Centraal Museum, Utrecht, The Netherlands
- 'Passion for Art – 35th Anniversary of the Essl Collection', Essl Museum of 'Contemporary Art', Klosterneuburg, Austria
- 'Framed – The Art of the Portrait', Art Gallery of Hamilton, Ontario

2006 – 'Aftershock – Contemporary British Art 1990–2006', Guangdong Museum of Art, Guangzhou, China and Capital Museum, Beijing
- 'Six Feet Under – Autopsy of Our Relation to the Dead', Kunstmuseum Bern, Switzerland
- 'Diagnosis (Art) – Contemporary Art Reflecting Medicine', Kunstmuseum Ahlen and Museum im Kulturspeicher, Wurzburg, Germany
- 'Light', Winchester Cathedral, Hampshire, United Kingdom
- 'Eretica', Museum Sant'Anna, Palermo, Sicily
- 'EGOmania – Just When I Think I've Understood...', Galleria Civica di Modena, Italy

2005 – 'Imagine a World', Bargehouse, London
- 'Wunderkammer – The Artificial Kingdom', The Collection, Lincoln, United Kingdom

- 'Art Out of Place', Norwich Castle Museum and Art Gallery, United Kingdom
- 'Ripe for Picking Fruits and Flowers', Jim Kempner Fine Art, New York
- '"Bock mit Inhalt" Summer Exhibition', Stedelijk Museum, Amsterdam
- 'Summer Exhibition 2005', Royal Academy of Arts, London
- 'London Calling – Y[oung] B[ritish] A[rtists] Criss-Crossed', Galleri Kaare Berntsen, Oslo
- 'Blumenstück – Künstlers Glück', Museum Morsbroich, Leverkusen, Germany
- 'The Body – Art & Science', National Museum, Stockholm
- 'Contemporary Photography and the Garden – Deceits & Fantasies', The Middlebury College Museum of Art, Vermont; The Parrish Art Museum, New York; Columbia Museum of Art, South Carolina and Tacoma Art Museum, Washington

2004 – 'Slimvolume 2004', Redux, London
- 'The Flower as Image – From Monet to Jeff Koons', Louisiana Museum, Humlebæk, Denmark
- 'The Synaesthetics of Art and Public', Gwangju Biennale, South Korea
- 'Lille Expo', Lille, France
- 'Garden of Eden', Helsinki City Art Museum
- 'The Garden of Delights, Galería Guereta, Madrid
- 'Flowers Observed, Flowers Transformed', The Warhol Museum, Pittsburgh
- 'Art of the Garden', Tate Britain, London; Ulster Museum, Belfast and Manchester Art Gallery
- 'Secrets of the '90s', Museum

voor Moderne Kunst Arnhem,
The Netherlands
– 'Flowers', Mary Boone Gallery,
New York
– 'Ideale e Realtà', Galleria d'Arte
Moderna di Bologna, Italy

2003 – 'Fourth Plinth Proposal', National
Gallery, London
– 'Fresh – Contemporary British
Artists in Print', Edinburgh
Printmakers
– 'Statements 7', 50th Venice Biennale
– 'Decembristerne', Gallery
Faurschou, Copenhagen
– 'Independence', South London
Gallery, London
– 'Genomic Issues', Graduate Center
Art Gallery, New York
– 'Bull's Eye – Works from the Astrup
Fearnley Collection', Arken Museum
of Modern Art, Ishøj, Denmark
– 'UnNaturally', Contemporary Art
Museum, University of South
Florida, Tampa; H & R Block
Artspace at the Kansas City Art
Institute; Fisher Gallery, University
of Southern California, Los Angeles;
Copia: The American Center for
Wine, Food and the Arts, Napa,
California and Lowe Art Museum,
University of Miami, Florida

2002 – 'Face Off', Kettle's Yard, Cambridge
– 'The Nude in Twentieth Century
Art', Kunsthalle, Emden, Germany
– 'Rapture – Art's Seduction by
Fashion Since 1970', Barbican
Gallery, London
– 'Thinking Big – Concepts for 21st
Century British Sculpture', Peggy
Guggenheim Collection, Venice
– 'The Rowan Collection –
Contemporary British and Irish
Art', Irish Museum of Modern
Art, Dublin

– 'Life is Beautiful', Laing Art
Gallery, Newcastle
– 'In the Freud Museum', Freud
Museum, London
– 'Iconoclash – Beyond the Image
Wars in Science, Religion and Art',
ZKM Center for Art and Media,
Karlsruhe, Germany
– 'Second Skin – Historical Life
Casting and Contemporary
Sculpture', Henry Moore Institute,
Leeds

2001 – 'Sacred and Profane', Mappin
Gallery, Sheffield, United Kingdom
– 'Printers Inc.', The Gallery,
Stratford-upon-Avon, United
Kingdom
– 'Summer Exhibition 2001', Royal
Academy of Arts, London
– 'Ohne Zögern', Weserburg Museum
of Modern Art, Bremen, Germany
– 'Metamorphosis and Cloning',
Foundation for Contemporary
Art, Montreal
– '/Arts', The Lux, London
– 'London Nomad', Beit Zeinab
Khatoun, Cairo Biennale
– 'Mind the Gap', Wetterling Gallery,
Stockholm
– 'Give & Take, Victoria and Albert
Museum, London
– 'Heads and Hands', Decatur House
Museum, Washington

2000 – 'Contemporary Art Trail', Wellcome
Wing, The Science Museum,
London
– 'Spectacular Bodies – The Art and
Science of the Human Body from
Leonardo to Now', Hayward Gallery,
London
– 'Conversation', Milton Keynes
Gallery, United Kingdom
– 'Out There', White Cube, London
– 'Psycho', Anne Faggionato, London

1999 – 'Skin', Deste Foundation, Centre
for Contemporary Art, Athens
– 'Something Warm and Fuzzy',
Des Moines Art Center, Iowa
– 'Into the Light – Photographic
Printing out of the Darkroom',
The Royal Photographic Society,
Bath, United Kingdom
– 'Officina Europa', Galleria d'Arte
Moderna di Bologna, Italy
– 'Now It's My Turn to Scream –
Works by Contemporary British
Artists from the Logan Collection',
Haines Gallery, San Francisco
– 'Presence', Tate Liverpool
– 'Spaced Out – Late 1990s Works
from the Vicki and Kent Logan
Collection', The CCA Institute,
California
– 'As Above, So Below – The Body's
Equal Parts', Fabric Workshop,
Philadelphia
– 'Physical Evidence', Kettle's Yard,
Cambridge

1998 – 'Family', Inverleith House, Royal
Botanic Garden, Edinburgh
– 'Group Exhibition', Galleri
Faurschou, Copenhagen
– 'Hope (Sufferance)', Sun and Doves
Gallery, London
– 'The Colony Room 50th Anniversary
Art Exhibition', A22 Projects,
London
– 'A Portrait of Our Times – An
Introduction to the Logan
Collection', San Francisco Museum
of Modern Art
– 'UK Maximum Diversity', Galerie
Krinzinger, Benger Fabrik Bregenz,
Austria
– 'Sam Taylor-Wood, Tracey Emin,
Gillian Wearing and Marc Quinn',
Galerija Dante Marino Cettina,
Umag, Croatia

– 'Inner Self', Mitchell-Innes & Nash, New York

1997 – 'The Quick and the Dead – Artists and Anatomy', Royal College of Art, London; Mead Gallery, University of Warwick, United Kingdom and City Art Gallery, Leeds

– 'Sensation', Royal Academy of Arts, London; Hamburger Bahnhof, Berlin and Brooklyn Museum of Art, New York

– 'The Body', The Art Gallery of New South Wales, Sydney

– 'Follow Me', Kunstverein Kehdingen, Freiburg, Germany

– 'A Ilha do Tesouro', Fundaçao Calouste Gulbenkian, Lisbon

1996 – 'Thinking Print – Books to Billboards 1980–95', Museum of Modern Art, New York

– 'Hybrid', De Appel, Amsterdam

– 'Mäfsig und gefräfsig – Künstlerinstallationen', MAK Museum für Angewandte Kunst, Vienna

– 'Works on Paper', Irish Museum of Modern Art, Dublin

– 'Happy End', Kunsthalle Düsseldorf

1995 – 'Time Machine', Musee Egizio, Turin

– 'Faith, Hope, Charity', Kunsthalle Wien, Vienna

– 'Contemporary British Art in Print', Scottish Museum of Modern Art, Edinburgh

– 'Ripple Across the Water', Minato Prefecture and Shibuya Prefecture, Tokyo

1994 – 'Life Is Too Much', Galerie des Archives, Paris

– 'Time Machine', British Museum, London

1993 – 'Prospect 93', Frankfurter Kunstverein and Schirn Kunsthalle, Frankfurt

– 'Sonsbeek 93', Arnhem, The Netherlands

– 'Young British Artists from the Saatchi Collection', Art Cologne

– 'Real Real', Vienna Secession

– 'Restaurant', Galerie Marc Jancou, Paris

– 'Young British Artists II', Saatchi Collection, London

1992 – 'The Boundary Rider, 9th Sydney Biennale', Art Gallery of New South Wales, Sydney

– 'London Portfolio', Karsten Schubert, London

– 'Strange Developments', Anthony d'Offay, London

– 'British Art', Barbara Gladstone Gallery, New York

1991 – 'Modern Masters', Grob Gallery, London

1990 – 'Group Show', Grob Gallery, London

– 'Hands', Grob Gallery, London

Awards

2004 – Fourth Plinth Commission for Trafalgar Square, London

2001 – The Royal Academy of Arts Charles Wollaston Award, London

Bibliography

Monographs and solo exhibition catalogues

– *Marc Quinn: Selfs* (Space, London and Foundation Beyeler, Riehen and Basel, Switzerland 2009)
– Self, Will, *Marc Quinn* (Gana Art Gallery, Seoul 2008)
– *Marc Quinn: Siren* (Space, London 2008); text by Germaine Greer; interview with the artist by Will Self
– Brotton, Jerry and Will Self, *Evolution* (White Cube, London 2008)
– Zeppetelli, John, Lynda Nead and Harvey Giesbrecht, *Marc Quinn* (DHC/ART Foundation for Contemporary Art, Montreal 2007)
– Oliva, Achille Bonito and Danilo Eccher, *Marc Quinn* (Electa Milan and Museo d'Arte Contemporanea Roma 2007)
– Mengham, Rod, Marc Quinn and Sue-An van der Zijpp, *Marc Quinn: Recent Work – Recent Sculpture* (Nai Publishers and Groninger Museum, Rotterdam 2006)
– Rogers, Richard, *Marc Quinn: Fourth Plinth* (steidlMACK, London 2006)
– Renton, Andrew, *Marc Quinn: Chemical Life Support* (White Cube, London 2005)
– Thomas, Rachael, Darian Leader and Susie Orbach, *Marc Quinn: Flesh* (Irish Museum of Modern Art, Dublin 2004)
– Marlow, Tim and Phillip Cribb, *Marc Quinn: The Overwhelming World of Desire (Paphiopedelium Winston Churchill Hybrid)* (Sculpture at Goodwood, United Kingdom 2003)
– Whitfield, Sarah, *Marc Quinn* (Tate Publishing, London 2002)
– Celant, Germano, Darian Leader and Marc Quinn, *Marc Quinn* (Fondazione Prada, Milan 2000)
– Leader, Darian, *Marc Quinn*

(Kunstverein Hannover, 1999)
– Juncosa, Enrique, *Marc Quinn Drawings* (Sala Amárica-Amárica Aretoa, Victoria, Spain 1999)
– Gisbourne, Mark, David Thorp, Will Self and Brian Eno, *Incarnate* (Booth-Clibborn Editions, London and Gagosian Gallery, New York 1998)
– Thorp, David, *Marc Quinn* (South London Gallery, London 1998)

General publications and group exhibition catalogues

– Hendy-Ekers, Kathryn, Lou Chamberlin and Deryck Greenwood, *Art-iculate: Art for VCE Units 1-4* (Cambridge University Press, Victoria, Australia 2010)
– Bonham-Carter, Charlotte and David Hodge, *The Contemporary Art Book* (Goodman, London 2009)
– Siebers, Tobin (ed.), *Zerbrochene Schonheit: Essays über Kunst, Asthetik und Behinderung* (Transcript Verlag, Bielefeld, Germany 2009)
– Cashell, Kieran, *Aftershock: The Ethics of Contemporary Transgressive Art* (I.B. Tauris & Co, London and New York 2009)
– Corginati, Martina, *L'Opera Replicante* (Editrice Compositori, Bologna, Italy 2009)
– Hood, Bruce, *Supersense: Why We Believe in the Unbelievable* (Constable & Robinson, London 2009)
– Hall-Duncan, Nancy, *Innovations in the Third Dimension: Sculpture in our Time* (Bruce Museum, Greenwich, Connecticut 2009)
– Graham-Dixon, Andrew (ed.), *Art: The Definitive Visual Guide* (Dorling Kindersley, London 2008)
– Ball, Mike, Margaret Tudge and Lin

Walker, *OCR Art & Design for AS/A Level* (Hodder Education, London 2008)
– Sirmans, Franklin (ed.), *NeoHooDoo: Art For A Forgotten Faith* (Menil Foundation, Houston 2008)
– Barozzini, Julie (ed.), *Art & Handicap* (Presses Universitaires de Namur, Belgium 2008)
– Rowan, Tiddy, *Art in the City: London* (Quadrille Publishing, London 2008)
– Ireson, Nancy, *Love* (National Gallery, London; City Museum and Art Gallery, Bristol and Laing Art Gallery, Newcastle 2008)
– Bonami, Francesco, *Arte Contemporanea, Volume Sei. Duemila* (La Biblioteca di Repubblica-l'Espresso and Electa, Milan 2008)
– Bernadelli, Francesco, *Arte Contemporanea, Volume Cinque. Anni Novanta* (La Biblioteca di Repubblica-l'Espresso and Electa, Milan 2008)
– Collings, Matthew, *This is Civilisation* (21 Publishing, London 2008)
– Gielen, Denis, *Atlas of Contemporary Art for Use by Everyone* (Museum of Contemporary Arts of Grand-Hornu, Boussu, Belgium 2007)
– Hall-Duncan, Nancy and Peter Sutton, *Contemporary + Cutting Edge: Pleasures of Collecting, Part III* (Bruce Museum, Greenwich, Connecticut 2007)
– Yukihiro, Hirayoshi and Tamaki Saito, *Skin of/in Contemporary Art* (National Museum of Art, Osaka 2007)
– Hammer, Martin, *The Naked Portrait* (National Galleries of Scotland, Edinburgh 2007)
– *Cass Sculpture Foundation 2004–2007* (Cass Sculpture Foundation, Chichester, United Kingdom 2007); texts by Stephanie Cripps, Amy Puttman, James Tregaskes and Kate Simms
– Mair, Robert and Rod Mengham, *Sculpture*

in the Close (Jesus College, Cambridge 2007)

– Oberhollenzer, Günther, Andreas Hoffer and Silvia Köpf, *Passion for Art: 35th Anniversary of the Essl Collection* (Edition Sammlung Essl, Vienna 2007)

– Hirst, Mark and Alistair Hicks, *Beyond Sensation* (Deutsche Bank Art Collection, London and Frankfurt 2007)

– Lullin, Etienne and Florian-Oliver Simm, *Contemporary Art in Print: The Publications of Charles Booth-Clibborn and his Imprint The Paragon Press 2001–2006* (The Paragon Press, London 2007)

– Mercurio, Gianni, Demetrio Paparoni and Davide Rampello, *Timer: Intimità/Intimacy* (Skira, Milan 2007)

– Sandell, Richard, *Museums, Prejudice and the Reframing of Difference* (Routledge, Oxford and New York 2007)

– Bracewell, Michael, Pi Li and Emily Butler, *Aftershock: Contemporary British Art 1990–2006* (The British Council, London 2006)

– Jones, Amelia, *Self/Image* (Routledge, London 2006)

– Imanse, Geurt, *Aanwinsten/Acquisitions 1993–2003* (Stedelijk Museum, Amsterdam 2006)

– Belliti, Chiara, *Eretica* (Civica Galleria d'Arte Moderna, Palermo, Italy 2006)

– Fibicher, Bernhard, *Six Feet Under* (Kerber Verlag, Bern, Switzerland 2006)

– Leismann, Burkhard and Ralf Scherer, *Diagnosis (Art): Contemporary Art Reflecting Medicine* (Wienand, Berlin 2006)

– Howgate, Sarah and Sandy Nairne, *The Portrait Now* (The National Portrait Gallery, London 2006)

– Richer, Francesca and Matthew Rosenzweig, *No.1: First Works by 362 Artists* (Distributed Art Publishers, Inc., New York 2005)

– Finckh, Gerhard, Alexandra Kolossa, Gerhard Graulich and Ute Riese,

Blumenstück – Künstlers Glück: Vom Paradiesgärtlein zur Prilblume (Museum Morsbroich, Leverkusen, Germany 2005)

– Dickins, Rosie, *The Usborne Book of Art* (Usborne Publishing, London 2005)

– Webster, Jeremy, *Wunderkammer: The Artificial Kingdom* (The Collection, Lincoln, United Kingdom 2005)

– Karin Altmann, *Figure Sculpture* (Sammlung Essl, Klosterneuburg, Austria 2005)

– Johannesen, Ina, Marianne Holtermann and Sarah Kent, *London Calling: Y[oung] B[ritish] A[rtists] Criss-Crossed* (Galleri Kaare Berntsen, Olso 2005)

– Ten Kate, Joke, Christien Oele and Hanna Vos-Niël, *Kunst en hulpmiddelen: de invalide mens verbeeld* (Nederlandse Veregniging Van Revalidieartsem, Amsterdam 2005)

– Holger, Lena (ed.), *Kroppen: Konst och vetenskap* (The National Museum of Fine Arts, Stockholm 2005)

– Doy, Gen, *Picturing the Self: Changing Views of the Subject in Visual Culture* (I.B. Tauris & Co, London and New York 2005)

– Kopp, Robert, Philippe Büttner and Ulf Küster, *Blumenmythos: Flower Myth* (Fondation Beyeler, Riehen and Basel, Switzerland 2005)

– Kelley, Mike, John Welchman and Christoph Grunenberg, *The Uncanny: Mike Kelley* (Walther Koenig, Cologne 2004)

– Guild, Trisha and Elspeth Thompson, *Private View* (Quadrille Publishing, London 2004)

– Padon, Thomas, *Contemporary Photography and the Garden: Deceits & Fantasies* (Harry N. Abrams and The American Federation of Arts, New York 2004)

– *Gwangju Biennale: a grain of dust, a drop of water* (Gwangju Biennale Foundation, South Korea 2004); texts by Yong-Woo Lee, Kerry Brougher, Milena Kalinovska,

Chika Okeke, Roberto Pinto, Won-il Rhee, Yoon-gyoo Jang and Chang-hoon Shin

– Kemp, Sandra, Alf Linney and Vicki Bruce, *Future Face: Image, Identity, Innovation* (Profile Books and The Wellcome Trust, London 2004)

– Bakker, Gijs and Renny Ramakers, *Design etc: Open Borders. Lille 2004* (Droog Design, Amsterdam 2004)

– *Stripped Bare: The Body Revealed in Contemporary Art* (Merrell Publishers, New York and London 2004); texts by Marianne Karabelnik, Victor Tupitsyn, Thomas Koerfer and Juri Steiner

– Tøjner, Poul Erik and Ernst Jonas Bencard, *The Flower As Image* (Louisiana Museum of Modern Art, Humlebæk, Denmark 2004)

– *Art of the Garden: The Garden in British Art, 1800 to the Present Day* (Tate Publishing, London 2004); texts by Martin Postle, Stephen Daniels, Nicholas Alfrey, Brent Elliott, Stephan Bann and Mary Horlock

– *Paratiisin Puutarha / The Garden of Eden* (Helsinki City Art Museum and Art Museum Meilahti, Finland 2004), texts by Berndt Arell, Jaako Heinimäki, Väinö Kirstinä, Tarja Halonen, Marika Hausen, Irma Savolainen, Leena Hämet-Ahti, Eeva Ruoff and Kaj Kalin

– Anker, Suzanne and Dorothy Nelkin, *The Molecular Gaze: Art in the Genetic Age* (Cold Spring Harbor Laboratory Press, New York 2004)

– Windsor, Alan, *British Sculptors of the Twentieth Century* (Ashgate Publishing, Aldershot, United Kingdom 2003)

– De Cruz, Gemma and Amanda Eliasch, *British Artists at Work* (Assouline, London 2003)

– Hwa Joo, Yeon, *British Contemporary* (Arario Gallery, Cheonan, South Korea 2003)

– Pavord, Anna, Andrew Moore and Christopher Garibaldi, *Flower Power:*

the Meaning of Flowers in Art 1500–2003 (Phillip Wilson Publishers, London 2003)
– Lombino, Mary-Kay and Philip K. Dick, *UnNaturally* (Independent Curators International, New York 2003)
– Meire, Mike, *Statements 7: The Overwhelming World of Desire* (Revolver Verlag, Frankfurt 2003)
– Von Herz, Juliane and Rudolf Schmitz (eds.), *Kunstgriffe* (Landesbank Hessen-Thuringen, Frankfurt 2003)
– Anderberg, Birgitte, Christian Gether and Gunnar B. Kvaran, *PLETSKUD Vaerker fra Astrup Fearnley Samlingen* (ARKEN Museum for Moderne Kunste, Ishøj, Denmark 2003)
– Gisbourne, Mark, *Face/Off: A Portrait of the Artist* (Kettle's Yard, Cambridge 2002)
– Hubbard, Sue and Ann Elliot, *Sculpture at Goodwood: A Vision for Twenty-First Century British Sculpture* (Sculpture at Goodwood, United Kingdom 2002)
– Miguel Fernandes Jorge, João, *Territórios Singulares na Colecção Berardo* (Sintra Museu de Arte Moderna – Colecção Berardo, Portugal 2002)
– Feeke, Stephen, *Second Skin* (Henry Moore Institute, Leeds 2002)
– Gerchow, Jan, *Ebenbilder: Kopien von Körpern – Modelle des Menschen* (Hatje Cantz, Ostfildern-Ruit, Germany 2002)
– Gillick, Liam, *White Cube: 44 Duke Street, St James's London* (Steidl, Göttingen, Germany 2002)
– Ottmann, Klaus, *Extreme Existence* (Pratt Manhattan Gallery, New York 2002)
– Latour, Bruno and Peter Weibel, *Iconoclash* (MIT Press, Cambridge, Massachusetts and ZKM, Center for Art and Media, Karlsruhe, Germany 2002)
– Hubert Pragness, *Invisible London* (Ellipsis, London 2001)
– Collings, Matthew, *Art Crazy Nation* (21 Publishing, London 2001)

– Milne, Julie, *Sacred and Profane* (Sheffield Galleries & Museum Trust, United Kingdom 2001)
– Marchant, Sandra Grant, *Metamorphosis and Cloning* (Musee d'Art Contemporaine, Montreal 2001)
– Blake, Peter, *Royal Academy Illustrated: Summer Exhibition 2001* (Royal Academy of Arts, London 2001)
– Nordenfelt, Amelie and Ebba Setterblad, *Mind the Gap* (Wetterling Gallery, Stockholm 2001)
– Kemp, Martin and Marina Wallace, *Spectacular Bodies* (Hayward Gallery, London and University of California Press, San Franciso 2000)
– Zweite, Armin, Doris Krystof and Reinhard Spieler, *Ich ist Etwas Anderes* (Kunstsammlung Nordrhein-Westfalen, Dusseldorf 2000)
– Naisbitt, John, *High Tech High Touch* (Broadway Books, New York 1999)
– Bevan, Rogar, *Now It's My Turn to Scream: Works by Contemporary British Artists from the Logan Collection* (San Francisco Museum of Modern Art, 1999)
– Joannou, Dakis, Katerina Gregos and Andrea Gilbert, *Skin* (Deste Foundation, Centre for Contemporary Art, Athens 1999)
– Lawrence, Rinder, *Spaced Out: Late 1990s Works from Vicki and Kent Logan Collection* (California College of Arts and Crafts, San Francisco 1999)
– Müller-Tamm, Pia and Katharina Sykora, *Puppen Körper Automaten: Phantansmen der Moderne* (Kunstsammlung Nordrhein-Westfalen and Oktagon, Dusseldorf 1999)
– Timms, Robert, Alexandra Bradley and Vicky Hayward (eds.), *Young British Art: The Saatchi Decade* (Booth-Clibborn Editions, London 1999)
– Stallabrass, Julian, *High Art Lite* (Verso, London 1999)

– Essl, Karlheinz, Rudi Fuchs and Heinz Tesar, *The Essl Collection: The First View* (DuMont Buchverlag, Cologne 1999)
– Ross, David and Gary Garrels, *A Portrait of Our Times: An Introduction to the Logan Collection* (San Francisco Museum of Modern Art, 1998)
– Muller, Brian, *UK Maximum Diversity* (Galerie Krinzinger, Vienna 1998)
– Wallis, Simon, *Physical Evidence* (Kettle's Yard, Cambridge 1998)
– Lynton, Norbert, *British Figurative Art Part 2: Sculpture* (Pale Green Press, London 1998)
– Faurschou, Luise and Jens Faurschou, *Janine Antoni, Wim Delvoye, Christian Lemmerz, Zbigniew Libera and Marc Quinn* (Galleri Faurschou, Copenhagen 1998)
– Buck, Louisa, *Moving Targets: A User's Guide to British Art Now* (Tate Publishing, London 1997)
– Bond, Anthony, *Body* (Bookman Press, Melbourne and The Art Gallery of New South Wales, Sydney 1997)
– Collings, Matthew, *Blimey! From Bohemia to Britpop: The London Artworld from Francis Bacon to Damien Hirst* (21 Publishing, London 1997)
– *Sensation: Young British Artists From The Saatchi Collection* (Royal Academy of Arts, London 1997); texts by Brooks Adams, Lisa Jardine, Martin Maloney, Norman Rosenthal and Richard Shone
– Schröder, Hans-Georg, *Follow Me* (Kunstverein Kehdingen, Freiburg, Germany 1997)
– Petherbridge, Deanna and Ludmilla Jordanova, *The Quick and the Dead: Artists and Anatomy* (University of California Press, Berkeley 1997)
– Molder, Jorge, Rui Sanches and Ana de Vasconcelos a Melo, *A Ilha do Tesouro* (Fundaçao Calouste Gulbenkian, Lisbon 1997)

– Cork, Richard and Penelope Curtis, *Breaking the Mould: British Art of the 1980s and 1990s: The Weltkunst Collection* (Lund Humphries, London 1997)

– Shand Kydd, Johnnie, *Spit Fire: Photographs from the Art World, London, 1996/97* (Thames & Hudson, London 1997)

– Burton, Jane, *The East Wing Exhibition: Contemporary Art at the Courtauld: October 1996 – July 1998* (Courtauld Institute of Art, London 1996)

– Haden-Guest, Anthony, *True Colours: The Real Life of the Art World* (The Atlantic Monthly Press, New York 1996)

– Syring, Marie Luise, *Happy End* (Kunsthalle Düsseldorf, 1996)

– Wye, Deborah, *Thinking Prints: Books to Billboards 1980–95* (Museum of Modern Art, New York 1996)

– Hurlimann, Annemarie, Birgit Mollik and Alexandra Reininghaus, *Mäßig und gefräßig: Künstlerinstallationen* (MAK Museum fur Angewandte Kunst, Vienna 1996)

– Lucie-Smith, Edward, *Art Today* (Phaidon, London 1995)

– Elliott, Patrick, *Contemporary British Art in Print: The Publications of Charles Booth-Clibborn and His Imprint The Paragon Press 1986–95* (Scottish National Gallery of Modern Art, Edinburgh and The Paragon Press, London 1995)

– Rainbird, Sean, *Emotional Detox* (Tate Publishing, London 1995)

– Watari, Koichi, *Ripple Across the Water* (The Watari Museum of Contemporary Art, Tokyo 1995)

– *Faith, Hope, Charity* (Kunsthalle Wien, Vienna 1995)

– Geissmar-Brandi, Christoph and Eleonora Louis (eds.), *Glaube Hoffnung Liebe Tod* (Kunsthalle Wien and Graphische Sammlung Albertina, Vienna 1995)

– Kent, Sarah, *Shark Infested Water: The Saatchi Collection of British Art in the 90s* (Zwemmer, London 1994)

– Kent, Sarah, *Young British Artists II* (Saatchi Gallery, London 1993)

– Brandt, Jan, Catelijne de Muynck and Valerie Smith, *Sonsbeek 93* (Snoeck-Ducaju & Zoon, Ghent, Belgium 1993)

– Ermacora, Beate, Bernhart Schwenk and Peter Weiermair, *Prospect 93* (Schirn Kunsthalle Frankfurt, Germany 1993)

– *Restaurant* (Galerie Marc Jancou, Zurich 1993)

– Gillick, Liam, *British Art* (Barbara Gladstone Gallery, New York 1992)

– Bond, Anthony, *The Boundary Rider* (Art Gallery of New South Wales, Sydney 1992)

Published by White Cube
on the occasion of:
Marc Quinn
Allanah, Buck, Catman, Chelsea,
Michael, Pamela and Thomas
7 May – 26 June 2010

Coordinated by Honey Luard
Editorial assistance by Dorothy
Feaver and Sara Macdonald
Designed by Stephen Coates
Printed by Granite

Artwork photography
The artist, Todd-White Art
Photography and Roger
Wooldridge

Artworks © the artist
Text © Mara Hoberman, Marc
Quinn and Joachim Pissarro
Catalogue © White Cube

Comparative illustrations
Page 98: © Carmen
Redondo/Corbis; page 100:
© Sandro Vannini/Corbis; page
103: © SuperStock/Getty Images;
page 104, left: © Walter
Geiersperger/Corbis; page 104,
centre: Philadelphia Museum of
Art/Corbis © ADAGP, Paris and
DACS, London 2010; page 104,
right: Marc Quinn; page 106, top
Marc Quinn; page 106, bottom:
© Paul Almasy/Corbis; page 107,
top: © Metropolitan Museum,
New York; page 107, bottom:
© Peter Willi/The Bridgeman
Art Library; page 109: © The
National Gallery, London

Joachim Pissarro is Bershad
Professor of Art History, Hunter
College and Director, Hunter
College Art Galleries, New York.
Mara Hoberman is Curator,
Hunter College Art Galleries,
New York.

The artist would like to thank
Pamela Anderson, Buck Angel,
Robin Astley, Dennis Avner,
Thomas Beatie, Juanita Boxill,
Alexandra Bradley, Franco
Cervietti, Chelsea Charms,
Stephen Coates, Lizzie Cross,
Bruce Dalzell Atherton, all at
Darbyshire, Joo Eun Bae, Jenny
Fairey, Christian Fernandez,
Daniela Gareh, Steve Haines,
Mara Hoberman, Ellie Howitt,
Jerry Hughes, Jay Jopling,
Rungwe Kingdon, Ömer Koç,
Adam Lowe, Honey Luard,
Sara Macdonald, all at MDM,
Steve Maule, Rafaella Pierotti,
Joachim Pissarro, Allanah Starr,
Graham Steele, Hisayo Tahara,
all at White Cube, Eric Wilcox,
Tony Wood and Jane Wilson.

Special thanks to
Georgia, Tiger, Lucas and Sky

ISBN: 978-1-906072-33-9

White Cube
48 Hoxton Square
London N1 6PB
T: +44 20 7930 5373
www.whitecube.com